ENTRIES FROM THE INTERIOR

ENTRIES FROM THE INTERIOR

SAMUEL HAZO

PITTSBURGH:
SERIF PRESS
2023

Serif Press

serifpress.com

This book is a gathering of notes, quotes and jottings drawn from over fifty years. I have read and valued the salmagundi and commonplace books of Elias Canetti, Joseph Joubert, E. M. Forster, Jose Saramago, Helen Bevington and others and have learned from all of them because each entry revealed what engaged a mind at the very moment of discovery and insight. I can only hope that this random gathering provokes similar awakenings.

For Janine Molinaro

Chinese proverb: "The only worthwhile words are those that improve upon silence."

Approximately five thousand years ago the Mesopotamians and Egyptians created hieroglyphics and cuneiform as their way of preserving the spoken word. The only conclusion that can be drawn from this is that the written word from the very beginning was a concession to history, to amnesia, to oblivion, to death itself. Without those markings or alphabets and the words they create, there would be no way to preserve for the eye what was originally intended for the ear. Alphabets are, therefore, simply a way of perpetuating a voice on a tablet or page. Yet there can be no doubt that the human voice, if not preferable to its re-creation in words of a page, certainly did precede it. In the beginning was the word, and the word was spoken. The writing down, like history, followed.

The French define lust as an excess of health, a kind of luxury—luxure. This seems true on the face of it. It is difficult to be sick and lusty.

Tomas Transtromer: "This is very motherly soup."

In *Stray Birds*, Tagore has a beautiful line: "His own mornings are new surprises to God."

Sloth is invariably considered by many as the mother of invention. Who, for instance, but a lazy man shortcutted his way to the wheel, the match, the boat? But sloth is also the father of mischief. Who but a lazy man opted for slavery?

As soon as people consider themselves in elitist terms, it's only a matter of time before they consider other people "inferior" or in need of "salvation" or simply "barbaric." It's also only a matter of time before these same people regard criticism as a form of persecution.

Loyalty to whom? Loyalty for what? I hear so much about loyalty, but loyalty remains, like courage, a blind virtue. One can be loyal to crime as faithfully as one can be loyal to one's country or one's family. One can be loyal to a lie as well as to the truth.

If a man has the power to kill another man, can he? Of course, he can. But does he have the right to use that power even if he has it? Of course not. The most important point is the right, not the power. But power, as history demonstrates time and time again, tends to make and be its own right. And that's the problem.,

Is it the fate of dictators to be statues toppled headless from their pedestals? Is it the destiny of saints and heroes to be shared and absorbed by their admirers?

Miguel de Unamuno wrote this intriguing paragraph: "Memory is the basis of individual personality, just as tradition is the basis of the collective personality of a people.

We live in memory and by memory, and our spiritual life is simply the effort of our memory to persist, to transform itself into hope, the effort of our past to transform itself into our future."

Lichtenberg has some interesting aphorisms. "A donkey appears to me like a horse translated into Dutch." "By reading so much we have contracted a sort of learned barbarism." "He kept continually polishing himself and finally became dull before he got sharp."

As the earth twirls around the sun, it cools. This coolness is what makes life possible on the surface, since it prevents our dying from heat. But the earth's core remains hot. This explains volcanoes and similar phenomena. We seem to mimic that it our very physiology. Under our skins we're all 98.6 degrees Fahrenheit. In atmospheric terms, that's sweltering.

I read recently that 50% of the inventions that will be in use ten years from now do not yet exist. This means that there is a wealth of inventive thought *to be thought* so that such inventions can be invented. I have no doubt that such thoughts will be thought and such inventions invented since the goal is the making of things destined for use. Utility is a strong magnet and an equally strong incentive. I wonder why the same energy cannot be bent toward liberal or speculative thought where the goal is not something to be used but something to be known for its own sake. I see the same dissimilarity in our attitude toward war and peace. We prepare passionately for war but much less passionately for peace. Who was it who said we could eliminate war if we brought the same passion to peace that we inexplicably bring to war?

Decades ago, I was invited to speak to a class of third graders about poetry. I decided instead to speak about the imagination, which is every poem's progenitor. Since much of any third grader's education involves learning the names of things ("learning the words for the world'), I thought it might be more interesting imaginatively if I asked them to assume that the world had not been named and that they had to create names for things. The one name that I vividly remember from that experiment was the name that one boy came up with for "bridge." He offered "shore-stapler," and that made "bridge" for me one of the dullest words in the language thereafter.

The same impulse to re-name things possessed me long after that while I was shuffling a deck of cards. I knew them all by name, of course, but I never thought about what the face of each card suggested to me. So, I began looking at each card in terms of what it prompted me to imagine, beginning with the joker. All I had to do was shuffle, cut and look, and some metaphor would suggest itself to me. I went through the entire deck that way with the following results.

Jokers. Each joker is God's jester. He turns cartwheels in the center of his world, swings tassels from his toes, bells from his cap, sees his name doubled down the margins of his kingdom, mixes well enough with all the numbers in the deck, knows he doesn't count and laughs it off

Deuces. Deuces are hearts in opposition, magnets never daring to touch, polar tips that turn the world between them, tug-of-war warriors tugging to a draw, two *pistoleros* who have paced off the distance between them but never turn to shoot, sisters in the same dress, sentries staring in different directions.

Threes. Threes are all that's left of a triangle that has lost its nerve and turned into a trio of black clovers or triplets from Guam. They have the look of coat buttons buttoned, two hearts heading south while one heads north, Shadrach, Meshach and Abednago, three pear halves lined in a dish, Melchior, Caspar and Balthasar, three brothers in their own parade.

Fours. All fours are thumbtacks holding up a map of nowhere, pillars of a building that will never be built, corners of tabletops, white fields with definite corners, a four-sided dragnet enclosing nothing, a basketball team whose center has been benched, quadruplets who have settled in the northeast, southwest, northwest and southeast of Colorado.

Fives. Five is the floor of the big top with four tent pegs planted for a spread tent and the main pole centered in its slot, five slugs in a bullseye, a quintet of jets in stunt formation, five geese veering in a pattern overhead, a perfect X if you draw the lines, gold stars in a cluster on the shoulders of the general of generals, all the pennies you need to make a nickel.

Sixes. Sixes are identical firing squads facing one another, spots for three railroad ties before the ties are positioned, paralleling lines of traffic, soldiers mustered in squads for inspection, a table set for six kings who will never arrive.

Sevens. Sevens are lucky because everybody says so. They forgive their brothers seven times seven times. They are Monday through Sunday again and again and again. They are the wonders of the world, the age of reason, the pillars of wisdom, the dwarves who saved Snow White, the winning dice.

Eights. Eights are hopscotch courts, deer prints in heavy snow, a string of islands somewhere in the South Pacific, a string of islands somewhere else, a spread of checkers at the ready, a hint of braids, two sets of quadruplets cribbed in a nursery.

Nines. Nine are eight kids picking on one in the middle, goal posts, perfect H's, telephone poles reflected in a river, a football scrimmage with the referee holding back both linemen and linebackers, vise heads converging on a wedge, tank tracks flanking a pothole, cross-stitches on a wound.

Tens. Tens are houses filled with all the children in the neighborhood, a pair of sculls passing buoys in a perfect tie, traffic seen from the thirty-sixth floor, expert needlework across an apron, machine-gun bullet nicks on plaster, eight men playing roulette at separate tables.

Jacks. Jacks are the juniors of the two-headed tribe. In profile or not, they are princes. They share stomachs in common. Their chests are festooned with tapestry. They sleep under a single blanket. The one-eyed jacks look slightly more willing to take chances. The full-faced jacks will be jacks forever.

Queens. Queens look like bridesmaids or ladies-in-waiting. They keep the peace between their husbands and their younger brothers. Their eyes have the wisdom of young grandmothers who see the whole picture all at once all the time. They're always smiling at something no one else finds funny. They're waiting for the kings to die so they can assume the throne.

Kings. Kings have forgotten how to smile. They are getting fat and know it. Once they were jacks, but they were slimmer then. They know what it means to wait. They've learned to curl their hair as well as their parted beards and the ends of their divided black mustaches. Their left hands hold axes and swords up to heaven like so many flags of warning. Their right hands wait for instructions.

Aces. Aces are the least and greatest of the whole kingdom. They are red and black suns centered in a sky without a cloud. They tell you they are kites in high winds, nightriders, kings of the hill, champions in all divisions, targets for marksmen who never miss. They have all the money in the world and more where that came from. They have the last, last, last, last word.

To see or to have seen? Which is preferable to most people? Usually the latter. So many people, for example, want to visit a place in order to have visited it or to meet a person in order to have met him or to read a book in order to have read it and so on. Such acts do not seem to be done for their own sake but are meant to be banked in memory. Perhaps it eases a kind of greed. Regardless, it is a way of forcing the present into the present perfect or the definite past. But it is obvious that to see in the present for the sake of seeing is a kind of fulfillment, not only for the eyes but for the mind as well. This is particularly true if what we see is someone or something we love. We want to keep seeing it in a kind of everlasting present, which seems to me about as close as we can come to what eternity really means. It is not a particular time in perpetuity. It is beyond time. Eternity is where time is not.

Baby shoes seem to be made unscientifically. No heels, no arches to speak of, and the soles are of the smoothest leather. And yet they are preserved by parents as sacred mementos as "Baby's first shoes."

There is a legendary story that describes what St. Francis Assisi did after he was approached by a prostitute, who invited him to spend the night with her. Francis was said to have smiled before he led her to a large fire. He entered the fire and invited the prostitute to join him. The prostitute refused and never again bothered him. I tried to capsulize the story in a short verse called "Lesson from Assisi."

> Consider Francis in the flames. The whore
> who tempted him would not make love in fire.
> Even if saints deserved some burning for,
> She thought the coals were sure to chill desire.
> Rebuked, the saint serenely baked on embers.
> The whore's good sense is what the world
>   remembers.

All this talk about progress.... My only definition of progress is whatever keeps us from degenerating. Sometimes progress simply may mean adhering to what are called past values because that is where it is assumed that true values are. Take the oath of Hippocrates, for instance. Doctors still swear by it and cannot improve upon it.

When Igor Stravinsky was in his last years, he was given to drawing female breasts on any sheet of paper at hand. Seeing him at his doodles, Robert Craft told him, "If you've seen one, you've seen them both."

John Henry Newman coined a good word for trendiness in education. He called it "viewiness."

It's one thing to hammer nails into a plank. It's something else to hammer nails into a living oak.

Moral evil is alleged to originate in the intention, whether the intention realizes itself in action or not. Moral good, however, is judged by the opposite standard. Good intentions are not regarded as consequential unless and until they realize themselves in action. Evil, therefore, seems to exist in the seed, good in the fruit.

At the trial of Yves Bouthillier, who was an official of the Vichy government that exploited the French people under its control, the presiding judge is reported to have noted with Gallic innuendo, "A minister of finance can always show the taxpayers that the burden which he imposes on them is light."

Christopher Fry defines a poem as "a poet's way of coming to terms with his own amazement."

Versatility in the animal world increases chances of survival, as in the case of the flying fox and the gibbon. But specialization or lack of versatility or adaptability almost guarantees extinction. The orangutan is the perfect example of this.

Sex is invariably a destructive force when separated from love and personality. When its only goal is private satiety, it is only a matter of time before it proceeds through a chromatic scale of pleasure for its own sake—promiscuity to masochism, masochism to sadism and so on.

I keep noticing the replacement of the real by the phony: faith by spiritualism, real evil by an exaggerated sense of the occult, history by sociology, art by artistry, intelligence by intellectuality, morality by moralizing, tone by noise, meritocracy by democratism, leisure by free time and so on.

Impressions: the way all dogs give themselves a total shake after a swim or a rain-soaking—the way a freight train seems to lengthen as it enters or emerges from a tunnel—a gathering of sparrows dogfighting for a morsel.

Because the explosion of a nuclear bomb could mean the end of life for man on this planet, it should be remembered that those who defend of the use of the bomb for deterrence or other "patriotic" reasons are not really on the side of man. American negotiators can say that the United States might lose one million lives after a first strike by the Soviets, but they invariably say that the Soviets would lose multi-millions in retaliation. This kind of argument is actually created by the bomb itself. It is the bomb itself that gives us this vocabulary and rhetoric. The voice of man is not heard.

Is sensory knowledge more memorable than empirical knowledge? Probably. The pain of a broken arm is a stronger memory than the square root of four.

The transitional phrase for television and radio broadcasters is "More after this." This could easily be the motto for the whole profession.

Adrian Mitchell said it: "Every poet wants all other poets to write the way he or she does—but worse."

Antonio Lobo Antunes: "...the camaraderie of war is a fellowship of false generosity resulting from a destiny suffered together but not really shared."

There was a nightclub in Antibes that was originally a restaurant with an attached bar. At the time when it was a restaurant, the owner decided to replace it with a disco lounge complete with technicolor lighting beneath a glass-block floor. Then he replaced the disco with a ring in which there would be nightly bouts with female boxers. The progression was obviously downward in order to keep the clientele interested. Then came topless dancers, then strippers, then sex acts on stage. Finally, it was sold for whatever could be salvaged from the property.

Poetry precedes religion historically and philosophically. Whatever is alive in religion is poetry. The rest is ritual.

A Greek saying: "When someone young dies, you have the duty to live twice as hard. The grief over death is something that only poetry can heal."

Joanna Richardson on Maurice Goudeket, Colette's third husband: "He had always been quick to break off relationships with women, because he was still keeping himself for the one, all-absorbing passion in which, deep down, he had ceased to believe."

Neanderthal man, who used tools and fire and always buried the dead, did not survive because he was allegedly too gentle. *Homo sapiens* survived through intelligence.

Fresh collie urine funneling in snow and steaming as orange as hot beer...

What's awesome in prospect can become trivial in retrospect. Anticipation heightens; memory lessens.

Photography mints memories. A photographer is a witness with tools. In our time the camera is accepted almost as a part of public dress. A man can walk in public with a camera strung from his neck and not be noticed. Not so for a painter with his easel.

In nature we find violence without malevolence, aggressiveness without valor. With humans, violence is often chosen, not from need, except defensively but from vindictiveness or malice. Animals kill to eat.

The word for vagina in French is *le vagin*. Curiously it's a masculine noun. The adjective in French that describes a woman with a sexy voice is *vaginale*.

Spencer thought that a tragedy was a "beautiful theory ruined by one ugly fact."

Man cannot love and kill at the same time. For man to kill, the impulse to love must be short-circuited so that all of the trust and sexual energy that buttress love and the act of love will henceforth go into killing as well as the mentality that makes killing possible. Sexuality is diverted into destruction. Our latent Puritanism even encourages this since Puritans regard the will as a kind of muscle, which explains why they distrust sexual relations since they believe that it weakens that muscle. In the act of loving, as Robert Hass notes, the will is more or less dissolved (subsumed), and Puritans cannot accept even a momentary dissolution, which is why Puritans regard sex as an evil—something that must exist as a concession to reproduction but otherwise avoided. The natural impulse to love, to lose oneself with and in the person loved, to give one's sexual energies an erotic and generative outlet was condemned, which of necessity diverted sexual energies into other channels. No wonder Puritans (and we are their progeny in many ways) have a latent history of cruelty and intolerance. This is the bounty of sexual energy perverted. We see the residue of this in our military, in the Puritanism of our work ethic, in many of our religious tenets and in our either-or attitude toward our political or national enemies. Carried even further, as Hass notes, the Puritan was to to turn sex into "an instrument of will, of the conscious cruelty that flowered in the writings of Sade." Whether or not the Puritans envisioned cruelty as an outcome of their philosophy is irrelevant. It was inevitable. Instead of being in awe of our sexual and mammalian nature, as William Blake was, the Puritan repressed it, thus stunting it in the bud as surely as anger stunts desire in the bud. The very act of love, the giving of self of lover and lover, is in the personal sense not simply a copulation, a union of penis and pubis, a matter of organs. It involves a subsumption of the will into the act itself—a subsumption that includes not only the will but the memory, the intelligence, the imagination, the nervous and digestive systems, the blood, the lungs, the fluids of the body—everything. When the hippies urged others to make love and not war, they were on to something whether they realized it or not. In fact, one must choose one or the other since one cannot do both simultaneously. If war wins out, as it usually does, the "soft laws" of love are put aside for a celibate soldiery (celibate in battle, at any rate) in the same spirit in which a boxer is required to avoid sexual intercourse while he is training for a bout. Note here how the puritanism of military and pugilistic training is almost identical—and for the same purpose. After the purpose is achieved, soldier and boxer are allowed to "resume." Sex is not seen for them as integral to love but simply as an appetite that requires satisfaction after weeks or months of suppression.

Proust: "When guilt vanishes, sensuality becomes lyricism."

Some differences between Hemingway and Picasso.... Hemingway seemed to have no philosophy of age. Aging to him meant losing one's instincts and appetites, suffering a decline in one's prowess, feeling one's talents and capabilities growing weaker and weaker. It's not surprising, therefore, that he took his own life rather than wait to be sentenced to death by it. Picasso, on the other hand, seemed to have a completely different attitude. He said or noted somewhere that it took him eighty years to learn to be young. Aging for him was a rediscovery (perhaps even a recovery) of youth. It brought not an abatement of his powers but an intensification. His face and body after his seventieth year seemed to contain the spirit of a younger man; his eyes especially have a certain directness and twinkle, even a hint of mischievousness about them. They are not like the eyes of most men at that age. This same look of mischief is confirmed by the numerous photographs of Picasso taken at that time—on the beach, breaking into a dance, making faces at the camera or just clowning around. In fact, some of his most erotic drawings he drew just before he died.

Three of our last most ferocious enemies in war have been Oriental (or Asian, to use the language of the politically correct). Is there a trace of racism in this, or is it merely history?

Caryl Phillips: "Hollywood's ability to leap deftly even the greatest hurdles of reality and create myths independent of place, time and facts, will always be its greatest strength."

If it is true that some of the Far Right do not wish to govern as much as they wish to rule, it helps explain much of their political behavior. Their spokesmen often seem to patronize their followers (as well as the electorate as a whole), not seeking to persuade or convince but to pronounce and declare. The assumption is that the public is an entity to be led, so why bother to inform or educate. Secretly they give the impression of either fearing or despising the very people who keep them in power. At their worst they believe in the political vaudeville of "bread and circuses." In our time this translates into promises of

wealth and that kind of spectacle associated with victories, athletic or military. It explains the lackeydom of their
loyalties, their servile gravitation to power while it is in
power. G. Gordon Liddy, for example, described his obedience to Nixon as subject to king. Oliver North said he
would stand on his head if his commander-in-chief ordered him to do it. This is the language and demeanor of
subjects, not citizens. No wonder such "subjects" are impatient with the democratic process. They lack the maturity and patience to work within it, and they, therefore,
never acquire the skill and understanding to deal with it.
It also explains their gravitation to the aristocracy of
money, since money in a capitalistic society is for them
synonymous with power.

Alan asks me when and how I make time to write. I answer that he would certainly make time whenever he and
his wife had amorous feelings for one another, wouldn't
he? He smiles and says yes, but he adds that it would not
be subject to revision.

The national switch from productive industries to service
or service-related industries is often a switch from the essential to the secondary. When countries cease to produce
their own steel or their own food and become the middle-
men or the mere users of the steel and food produced
elsewhere, they lose a great deal of their independence.

No matter what he wrote by hand, he always wrote like a
man who was practicing his signature.

John Ciardi: "A man is measured by what engages his attention." "Games are human activities made difficult for the joy of it."

Comment of a woman speaking frankly of a man she still hopelessly loves but who does not love her: "Love for me is like the bubble in the stem of a wine glass—a defect."

Octavio Paz: "Even to feel itself, the body seeks another body."

Alastair Reid: "Cats are unpunishable by nature."

Old beauty queens.... The older they get, the heavier the rouge, the more abundant the meant-to-be-distracting diamond rings, the snugger and wider the diamond or ruby necklaces around their turkey necks.

Alan McGloshon: "Carnival is a phenomenon of cultured societies. Primitive man had no need of it, for the return of chaos loomed over him every hour of his life. But as soon as men began to create for themselves conditions of stability and some measure of the rule of reason, at once the necessity for the compensating period, however brief, of anarchy and license became manifest. In all ages and in all parts of the earth...the most intelligent societies have recognized this need and tried to canalize it, to contain it within specified dates of their local calendar."

Rivers are verbs. Lakes are nouns. Oceans and seas are gerunds.

Suffering and pain have no past and no future. They just are.

As cold as a dime dropped on the sidewalk in January.

To hatchet off the head of a hen and then let it run head-less around the yard until the bloodied, pulsing body fi-nally turns dead...

The dogs and sparrows were moving up a one-way street the wrong way. It made the street seem wrong.

As a teacher I'm not concerned with extra-sensory or supra-sensory perception. Sensory perception is enough.

Photographed, I lose my third dimension. Sculpted, I'm lifeless in likeness. Recorded, I persist as sound without a mouth or breath or memory.

Since the end of Vatican II, the Catholic Church has been urging men to put the morality of their acts to the arbitra-tion of their consciences. Yet this same church insists that it is the ultimate moral authority. Are these claims mutu-ally exclusive? How, for instance, can a person yield his conscience to authority while simultaneously respect the authority of his own conscience? I do not deny that a per-son may reach a conscientious decision that may coincide with a particular moral position of the church, but that is not the same as having that position molded in advance. In studying literature, one does not read a criticism (authori-tative or not) of a book before one has read the book and come to certain literary conclusions of one's own. These conclusions may or may not coincide with "authoritative" or "traditional" ones. Likewise, there are certain geometry texts that contain a sheaf of answers at the end of the book. I know students (I was one myself) who would consult the answer-sheaf before trying to solve the problem by themselves. The actual creative drama of working out the problems by themselves was sacrificed. Too many Catholics still have this mentality. They want to know the answers before they know the questions, and they fail to realize that in matters of belief and morality there are some questions that have more than one answer or, in some cases, no answers at all.

Albert Camus wrote that the "decadence of Greek sculpture and the dispersion of Italian art began with the appearance of smiles and expressions in the eyes, as if beauty ended where the mind begins."

I learned somewhere that Hitler himself chose red, black and white as the colors of the Nazi flag: red for blood, black for death and white for nothing.

Every writer should take to heart these words of Ernest Hemingway: "I found the greatest difficulty, aside from knowing truly what you really felt...was to put down what really happened in action; what the actual things were which produced the emotion that you experienced."

What is applause but noise—pleasant noise but noise nonetheless.

Herman Hesse has always impressed me as a writer whose reputation has exceeded his talent, but there is one statement of his that seems irrefutably true: "I believe that for all its patent absurdities life nevertheless has a meaning. I resign myself to being unable to find this ultimate meaning with my reason, but I am prepared to serve it even if it means sacrificing myself...Such faith cannot be commanded, we cannot force it upon ourselves. We can only experience it. Those who cannot do that seek their faith in the church or in science or in patriotism or socialism, or in some quarters where there are ready-made moralities, programs and prescriptions."

When someone you love dies, the person you were with him or her—the person he or she created in yOu when you met or talked—dies as well.

Someone should write an essay on the difference between universality and notoriety. For a poem to be universal it must in and of itself establish communion between what it is and what all men believe to be true. Notoriety is no more than recognition. It is usually ascribed to persons, but poems may be said to have it and yet lack universality. Notoriety is a mile wide and an inch deep.

The tenses of the mind are past, present and future. The tense of the body and its hungers is now.

It is sobering to know that someone is murdered, mugged, kidnapped or raped every six minutes in Dallas, Texas.

The body's primary impulse is to go on. The mind's primary impulse is to make sense out of the going on. The final enemy of the body is death. The mind, knowing in advance that death is inevitable, tries to make sense even out of that.

When a jet climbs to its cruising altitude, it angles sleekly upward through dense, dirty clouds like a submarine surfacing swiftly in an emergency.

The more protracted and widespread the pressure or the disaster, the deeper and more inevitable and ineluctable the sense of solidarity among the victims. Take the threat of short rations, for example. At first, those threatened with scarcity might seek to provide for themselves by squirreling away supplies. But once the supplies are depleted, these same people would tend to see themselves facing a common threat and attempt to pool their resources with others. But why does this sense of commonality happen usually when people have no other choice.

In literature, in art, in architecture, in personality itself there must be present a sense of space. If there is only a sense of confinement, of spacelessness, then literature, art, architecture and personality are earthbound, weighted by a heavier gravity than gravity, incapability.

Who was it who said that psychology is the religion of the twentieth century? J. H. Plumb has noted that history (the attempt to find roots of the present in the past) may be replaced by social sciences (latitudinal studies). Robert Penn Warren added a corollary to this, noting that only by penetrating the past and attempting to understand it can man discover the humanity of history. He concluded that this act tends to make man truly human. Without a sense of the past, man simply becomes a mechanism, which is how the social sciences regard him.

The art of Islam is a lived-with art. Thus, the emphasis in their art on jewelry, rugs, inlaid table tops and so on.

The magician's crepe handkerchief came parachuting to the floor. When it hit, it billowed briefly and fractured like smoke caught in a downdraft.

Once you are a parent, you are on duty forever.

No center knows that it's a center.

Camus is to twentieth century literature and thought what Lincoln is to nineteenth century American history. Unavoidable.

Every poet is really Icarus. He is drawn to dare impossibility even if this means he might fail in the attempt. His fate is to try to give a voice to silence, to let what cannot speak somehow speak through him. His victory, if it comes, must of necessity be a victory of the moment, a kind of lyric triumph. Transcendence is the goal. The historian and the philosopher tend to become soberer, even more somber, with age—as if the weight of reality and the necessity of knowing and understanding it were too much. On the other hand, the poet concedes to reality in advance its ultimate pindown, its ability to crush, but he tries to transcend it en route. That is why the poetic character of a people is often revealed by how much they value and respond to the epiphany of a poem, a song, a toast or even a curse before they, like Icarus, fall from the heights of that same moment.

He put his weight on his right foot so that his sole-print and heel-print punctuated the sand. He watched as the wind slurred and sorted the loose sand until, within minutes, there was no footprint at all, not even an echo of it.

Is it possible to remember the future? Can't memory be anticipatory as well recollective? If so, can't there be a poetry that tells us what we may yet know?

My days are wars on isms.

My shadow is all I concede to midnight.

The adjectives used to describe prominent men in previous eras tend to reveal those qualities most prized and respected by the societies that used them like wily Ulysses, pious Aeneas, the prudent wife, emperors or popes described as "the good" or "the august" or "the merciful." What adjectives do we use in our era? Pragmatic, clever, shrewd, smart, aggressive, popular?

Festschrift. Words for a festival.

Sansculottist. A revolutionary (literally he who is without culottes or knee britches).

A couch awaits its sitters, a hat its head, a glove its hand.

It is important never to lose faith in the power of truth, never to equivocate or accede to impatience or violence when you do not see the truth prevail. Because there is no substitute for the truth and no alternative to it, it will prevail eventually. You simply cannot lose faith in it so that you will be worthy of the truth when it does prevail.

Gothic alphabets look liturgical, sacred, almost holy. Why?

Vertical, horizontal or askew, a book on a shelf always seems to be saying, "Read me."

Victory means domination. Domination is from *dominari* (to be lord and master), which in turn is from *dominus* (lord). Hence, to dominate means to lord over. It is an appeal to pride. Defeat, therefore, means to be subjected to the pride and will of the victor. Eventually the defeated yearn to dominate their dominators as a way to free themselves from domination. And the cycle continues.

Houses at night seem to talk to themselves in squeaks and moans and shiftings like old men mumbling to themselves as they turn in their sleep.

Nancy Barkman said this to me after she read a book of my poems, "You give me permission to feel what I feel. You legitimatize my feelings."

Flowers are stills in motion.

The way we dress and arm ourselves for work and then do the reverse for sleep is taken for granted by most of us. There is even a code of dress for sleep, which is a code for one third of every day and every life.

There is a big difference between aging and decay.

Tired shirts. Tired ties.

Journalists, especially television journalists or those who think like television journalists, are constantly saying or implying that the public's attention span is short or that the public may be surfeited on such-and-such an issue. Consequently, by catering to one or the other of these estimates of the quality of public attention or public appetite, the profound as well as the superficial aspects of history are relegated to the same oblivion. Vietnam and its causes are forgotten. Nixon is forgotten. Iran-Contra is forgotten and so forth. Could it be that these propensities are attributable to the journalists' voluntary amnesia or attention spans? A genuine historian, for example, whose attention should presumably be no smaller than time itself, would never make such a statement without convicting himself of inexcusable superficiality. The historian must be able to separate the significant from the evanescent. The assumption of the deadline journalist is that everything becomes yesterday's news. But because the seeds of today and tomorrow derive from yesterday, the significant events of the past must be understood and kept in mind whether the public is bored with hearing about them or not. The important remains important because it is important.

John Berger in G. "The wife so values the time still left to her that she is desperate to fill it with new experience. The widow so despises the time still left to her that she is certain that no true experience can enter it. Both are deceived." "When Zeus, in order to approach a woman he had fallen in love with, disguised himself as a bull, a satyr, an eagle, a swan, it was not only to gain the advantage of surprise; it was to encounter her (within the terms of these strange myths) as a stranger. The stranger who desires you and convinces you it is truly you in all your particularity whom he desires, brings a message from all that you might be, to you as you actually are. Impatience to receive that message will be almost as strong as your sense of life itself. The desire to know oneself surpasses curiosity. But he must be a stranger, for the better you, as you actually are, know him, and likewise the better he knows you, the less he can reveal to you of your unknown but possible self. He must be a stranger. But equally he must be mysteriously intimate with you, for otherwise instead of revealing your unknown self, he simply represents all those who are unknowable to you and for whom you are unknowable. The intimate and the stranger.... From this contradiction in terms...is born the great erotic god which every woman in her imagination either feeds or starves to death."

Intellectual slavery is a term that applies to all those people who simply accede to whatever is happening, make no effort at all to understand or judge what is happening and then just let it wash over them like water. They always act as if it does not involve them directly or, if it does, there is nothing they can do but accept it. They see history as something apart from themselves. They do not see history

as something they make or have any influence over whatever.

So many British singers, though they speak with British
accents, sing with American accents. Do they do this because the market for their music is in the United States?
Do they tailor their accents to the market? Or have they
simply concluded that the American style of singing popular songs is the standard? Do they see any discrepancy between their being British while "singing American?" What
would be the reaction if an American singer in France,
Spain or England sang with a French, Spanish or British
accent?

T. S. Eliot: "In the end, a work of art makes its own audience."

It is often (but incorrectly) assumed that abundance coun-
teracts greed and that those with much want less. But the
reverse is often true, and it is usually explained by the
maxim "The more you have, the more you want." True
though this may be, there is another aspect of greed that
manifests itself in the desire of those with abundance to
want to lose less, to preserve what they have without any
loss whatever. It disguises itself as "savings."

For years the Democratic Party was identified as the party
of and for working people. It appealed to laborers and job
holders. It was the opposite of entrepreneurs—those with
enough money (capital) to enable others to work for them.
In the seventies the party seemed to shift its concern from
labor to the to the interests to individual groups—small in

some cases, larger in others. These groups were identified by gender, race, ethnicity or sexual orientation. The result was and is that these groups took precedence over the laboring class as a whole. Had the Democratic Party concentrated on the many in their traditional manner, the benefits would have accrued to the few as well.

As much as I admire the erudition of T. S. Eliot and W. H. Auden, I think that neither could write a poem like Gabriel Celaya's "*Poesia Es un Arma Cargada de Futuro*" ("Poetry Is a Weapon Loaded with the Future"). Celaya's poem is charged with a true patriotic passion. The talent to articulate passion is absent in the poetry of Eliot and Auden as it is absent in much contemporary British and American poetry.

Lewis Lapham: "Freedom of thought brings societies the unwelcome news that they are in trouble, but because all societies, like all individuals, are almost always in trouble, the news doesn't cause them to perish. They die instead from the fear of thought and from the paralysis that accompanies the silencing of opinions that contradict the official wisdom."

The desire to legalize things is rampant, i. e., legalized gambling, legalized abortion, legalized marijuana etc. The perception seems to be that legalization makes everything okay, legally speaking. Take war, for example. Seemingly outlawed, it happens. Because it happens, laws and rules like the Geneva Conventions are adopted to govern how war can be waged in a "civilized way." The use of poison gas is outlawed. But it remains legal to bomb—even to bomb nuclearly. Absurd.

Elias Canetti: "In the long run all secrets which are confined to one faction, or still more, to one man, must bring disaster, not only to the possessor, but also to all concerned; every secret is explosive, expanding with its own inner heat."

Thornton Wilder: "Cruelty is a failure of the imagination."

John Ciardi: "I have, to be sure, had things I wanted to say about society and its quirks and failures. I count it a blessing that for twenty years I wrote a column for *The Saturday Review* and was free to sound off on any cause and cantanker. But I have learned not to send a poem on a prose errand." "The craft (of poetry) is not easy. It is better than easy. It is joyously difficult."

John Ciardi was once shown a copy of *The Obituary Journal*. The person who showed him the magazine added that anyone could submit his or her own obituary and that it would be printed. Ciardi thumbed quickly through the magazine and handed it back to its owner, adding, "I am sure it will be followed by *Son of Obituary Journal*."

Ezra Pound: "Read seeds, not twigs."

Amos Oz: "Through most of histories of the Jews have usually adopted two spiritual reference points: the distant, glorious past and some sort of distant messianic future. The present and the immediate future were almost always

viewed as a 'vale of tears' whose tribulations could be be-
moaned but not acted upon accordingly, it was considered
pointless to spend too much emotional energy on them. It
was assumed that when the Messiah came, he would bring
about the exalted future—thus renewing the marvelous
past and at the same time dissipating the troubles of the
present."

"I see it feelingly," says Gloucester after Lear proclaims, "...
you see how the world goes." To see something "feelingly"
means that the experience is more than ocular; it touches
the human core within us that makes us worthy to be
what and who we are. Likewise, to know something "feelingly" is not to know it in the abstract but to know it as it
is—with the same sense of reality that we have about our
very selves. If we do not see and know in this way—if we
prefer the easy knowledge of abstraction—if we settle for
part of the truth instead of the whole of it, are we not the
same as liars?

Wright Morris: "Much of my fiction grew out of my need
for an experience I came too late for."

Keystone...the crowning stone in an arch that makes the
arch possible.

George Steiner: "Originality is antithetical to novelty."

Poetry is the marriage of thought and feeling—felt
thought or what Jacques Maritain called "intelligenciated
feeling." It is not present in verse. There is always much
verse that has pretensions of being poetry but is really

just verse. It is characterized by facility, that's all. It takes a certain knack to write it, but it's an acquirable knack. Poetry on the other hand is born of inspiration—a gift.

Think of a story of a married but childless woman who feels maternal toward a wayward young man of eighteen. He is cynical and selfish enough to see that the woman's need to love him as a surrogate son is real, and his cleverness permits him to take advantage of it and exploit it. Imagine the sadistic selfishness of this. Imagine the pain and agony of the woman who must endure this abuse because she is unable to withdraw her affection for him since she needs to give it in order to feel complete.

Jacques Barzun: "Great populations without a god outside themselves will turn to national war or race hatred to find the glow of common sacrifice and the call to transcendence that the human spirit requires."

A baseball game is observed as it happens, but it is best understood in retrospect. An inning that is just starting is fraught with possibilities; the same inning remembered is not. A baseball manager's strategies for the game offer a choice of many possibilities, but facts make strategies obsolete. That's when understanding begins. It involves looking back or looking into. Thinking and then acting is in the present tense. Understanding is historical.

Woman, not man, is the authentic mammal. Her very appearance is mammalian, particularly when she is in motion in the water. It is the female who has the glands that are truly and functionally mammary while these same glands in the male are underdeveloped. They almost seem like a symbolic afterthought.

Who says we have to imagine the nightmare of a nuclear war or explosion? Both have already happened—twice in Japan, once in Chernobyl.

To wave goodbye is to speak. The wave may even be more eloquent than the word. The French seems to favor the eloquence of silence. They say that there are two silent goodbyes for the French—one with the hand, one with the hat.

Hunter S. Thompson: "In a closed society where everybody's guilty, the only crime is getting caught. In a world of thieves, the only sin is stupidity."

St. John Perse: "Even religions are born of the need for poetry, which is a spiritual need."

Consider the cults that have been created by the deaths of James Dean, Elvis Presley, John Lennon and others. Isn't the existence of such groups reminiscent of the same phenomenon that makes certain children reluctant to give up the breast? Having become inured to the nipple, they are reluctant to eat, as it were, on their own thereafter. Similarly, these same cultists, having fed on the popularity of their chosen gods as the sources of their sustenance cannot accept the fact of their deaths. So, they begin chanting "James Dean lives!" or "Elvis lives!" and so on.

In this same connection what about the ongoing symptoms of protracted and accepted immaturity that characterize some films and numerous popular singers and musicians in performance? In film after film many of the basic conflicts are not settled or even considered for resolution but are overwhelmed by shouting, fist fights or the use of weapons. There is something adolescent about all this. At song festivals the crescendo of decibels eventually reaches the level of pure noise.

Justice William O. Douglas: "They deplored the fact that man was being more and more regarded only as a biological or economic being. He was put into tables and polls and considered as fungible as wheat or corn. One of them made the point that there was a diminishing recognition of the spiritual qualities—of the importance of quickening man's conscience and asking him to search his soul as well as his mind for answers to the perplexing questions of the day. Perhaps man was losing his freedom in a subtle manner. He was becoming more and more dependent on other men. Part of that dependency was necessary since man had to look to others for his food and fuel and essential services. But he also had to become dependent on others for his entertainment and for his ideas. He looked to people rather than to himself and the earth for his salvation. He fixed his expectations on the frowns or smiles or words of men, not on the strength of his own soul, or the sunrise, or the warming south wind, or the song of the warbler. Once man leaned that heavily on people, he was not wholly free to live. Then he became moody rather than self-reliant. He was filled with tensions and doubts. He walked in an unreal world, for he did not know the earth from which he came and to which he would return. He became a captive of civilization rather than an adventurer who topped each hill ahead for the thrill of discovering a new world. He lost the feel of his own strength, the power of his own soul to master any adversity."

A newspaper man's criticism of George F. Will's book on baseball, *Men at Work*: "It is literate beyond its subject matter."

Healthy, we glory in our individuality. Sick, we realize our dependence on others.

No matter when you look at flowers, they are always saying hello.

The way a woman towels herself after swimming—first, with eyes shut, the face, the ears, the nape, then each arm and armpit separately, then the upper halves of the breasts, then with downward strokes the inner thighs, then the loins, then one by one the legs from buttocks to feet, and, finally between the toes before she stands for the last dabbings behind the ears and then within the ears themselves, then the back of the neck, and done.

The smell of applewood burning.

Thomas Hardy: "Literature is the written expression of revolt against accepted things."

A perched toad, breathing like a bladder, in pulsations...

Hearing something a hundred times is not as good as see-ing it once.

The country of false truth.

Time is a constant tyranny. It broods over our happiness, reminding us that all comes to an end eventually. It is like a weight on us when we are sick. Either way we are sub-ject to its ineluctable chronologies. It governs the cycle of days, weeks, months and years. It is the clock of aging that begins to tick the instant we are born. It answers us when we ask how long it will take to arrive wherever. No won-der we seek to free ourselves from its tyranny by doing things where time seems to be suspended—sports, trips, love-making. I would suggest that reading a novel or a poem or seeing a play or a film is a way of entering a dif-ferent time zone. Hours and years can be condensed there. The clocks are sprung, and the pendulums of the imagina-tion take over.

Yakub Ibn Ishak al-Kindi (an Arab Islamic philosopher of the ninth century): "We should not be ashamed to ac-knowledge truth and assimilate it from whatever source it comes to us, even it is brought to us by former generations and foreign peoples. For him who seeks the truth, there is nothing of higher value than truth itself; it never cheapens or abases him who searches for it, but ennobles and hon-ors him."

The great majority of those who speak on television speak as conclusionists. In short, they pronounce. They present audiences with pre-thought or pre-written conclusions, be they headlines or so-called commentary or "expert opinions." There is almost a total absence of speculative thought, i.e., thought for its own sake in the quest for truth. Television does not leave time to learn—time to think one's way out of confusion of doubt. The fact that time on television costs money explains this stringency to a great degree. It is the exact opposite of what happens to time in a real discussion or in a genuine seminar when we proceed wherever the discussion leads.

So many Christians think of life only as pre-death.

Born of Calliope, Orpheus was the son of a muse.

What the American public needs periodically is a good dose of disillusionment. Optimism and good wishes do not create the environment where truth can be sought for truth's sake and accepted. Disillusionment often erases everything that was once thought to be true. It's like the disillusionment that someone experiences when a certain custom or a masterpiece or a seemingly settled tradition is shown for what it is. When the disillusioned person realizes this and starts re-thinking, he then really begins to learn. Disillusionment creates the possibility of renewal.

How can partial people have a total view of anything? Poetry is making something out of something else. Poems are made out of words, jams are made out of strawberries or peaches, wines out of grapes, clothes out of wool and cotton, songs and speeches out of our inhaled breath.

Richard Nixon—an unsavory, paltry man who appealed to unsavory, paltry people.

Given the choice between romance and reality or between personability and personality, the public will almost always choose the romantic and the personable. Consider Ronald Reagan.

A cloud of birds.

One can speak factually about the past because it has happened. One can speak conditionally about the future because it might happen. But of the present—the time being—what can be said? How can one talk or write about what's here if what's here is passing even as you talk or write? There is no fixed present. What we call the present is in flux. Anticipate it, and it's here. Here, it's already passing.

One of the most controversial things a writer could do in the United States was to be critical of Israel. Until recently, this applied to criticism of any aspect of Israeli policy toward Palestinians and Palestine. Calling such criticism anti-Semitic was the standard retort. Robert Fisk has correctly identified this as Israel's "moral immunity" in the United States. In the past decade this has changed among American Jews. The Jewish Voice for Peace, for example, has taken public issue with many of the policies of the Israeli government, particularly in the Netanyahu era. It has shown that many of these policies are simply contrary to Judaism and are truly anti-semitic.

Stephen Spender once asked T. S. Eliot if "The Wasteland" prefigured the end and collapse of civilization. Eliot said that it did. Spender then asked him how it would end. Eliot said it would end with people killing one another in the streets.

Abraham Lincoln claimed that we cannot escape history. Yet in the working of government, on television and in city planning, the impulse always seems to incline toward an avoidance or an indifference to history. Events are seen as subsequential, not consequential. The emphasis is on the episodic, not the dramatic. Years are disconnected from years, decisions from effects, acts from their results. It should be noted that the episodic in literature is regarded as the weakest form of narration since its only continuity is the continuity of the same character in different circum-stances at different times. On the contrary, dramatic unity is based on the consequences of actions by a character, and these actions have moral dimensions. The latter view is deeper, often ironic and more life-like. The former is not.

Louis Pasteur: "Chance favors the prepared mind."

Panjandrum—muckamuck—a person of some impor-tance, i.e., a panjandrum in a bookstore.

Earned money versus luck-money. Earned money is money gained from work. It's what I call "sweet money." Luck-money that comes from gambling or inheritance is disassociated from work. Its mother is what used to be called "fortune" or pure luck. Depending on the person so favored, it can have beneficial or disastrous consequences. I know one lawyer who represented eight people who had won the Pennsylvania lottery. He said that winning had ruined the lives of all eight of them.

Antoine de Saint-Exupery: "When you bring imagination to bear on the present, then you have great poetry. Like Dante." "Life has taught me that there is only one true kind of courage: resisting the condemnation of a mode of thought."

Psychological collapse (nervous breakdown) often occurs when a sane mind is confronted by an absurd situation, i.e., war.

Even in *flagrante delicto* the porpoise continues smiling.

Looking up at clouds, you might say they interrupt the sky. Looking down, you would say they interrupt the earth and leave it spottily imprinted with their ephemeral shadows.

If reading is an addiction, I'm one of the addicted. I read daily because I need to. My eyes, my mind and my very soul need the daily fix of print, and as a teacher for many years I not only encouraged but required students to read. I own more books than I have shelves for, and I remind myself, as one friend once told me, that all books were people once. And always will be. Robert Louis Stevenson said once that a man cannot consider himself educated until he is stranded between train connections at a railroad station and knows no one and does not have a book in his possession and yet is not bored for a minute. I've applied that test to myself, and I have to admit that I don't rank high among the non-bored, book or no book.

The quiet food of books.

Georges Perec: "They lived in a prison of plenty where the ultimate in opulence was to be able to light your corona with a fifty-dollar bill."

The way the tide surrenders in white murmurs to the shore...

There is a difference between inhabitants and residents. Inhabitants are permanent dwellers and have a history of being permanent dwellers. Residents in many cases have the smell of transients.

"Silvia...whose beauty was so great that any person who received her smiling gaze would feel himself short-lived and mortal."

John Ciardi: "It is the fixed dementia of the military mind that troops can be made enthusiastic by being ordered to shout."

Now that we seem to have become a nation constantly at war, all the old and perhaps timeless clichés about our enemies and allegiances are heard, i.e., "These people understand nothing but force." "We must give our unquestioning support to the President." "We must support the troops and thank them for their service." "Protesters have no right at all to protest." Now that military service is no longer compulsory, the young men and women in the various services are essentially seen as employees who are expected to do what they are trained and paid to do when ordered to do so. Any dissent is usually dismissed by asking the dissenters, "You understood what you were volunteering for, didn't you?" Among those in higher command in all the services, those in the armed forces are often referred to simply as assets. Based on how the Army, Navy and Marine Corps have been used in the first decades of the twenty-first century, I find certain similarities between the members of these branches and the French Foreign Legion. Legionnaires were also volunteers, and they dutifully served wherever they were ordered to serve. No dissent was tolerated.

John Berger: "Poetry makes language care because it renders everything intimate. There is often nothing more substantial to place against the cruelty and indifference of the world than this caring."

Being blind literally means being unable to see. But isn't it possible to call any of the other senses blind when they are unable to do what they exist to do? Hands that do not feel could be considered blind. In fact, the body as a whole when no longer able to function is in this sense blind.

As we age, we quibble. Women leak, and men dribble.

We secrete through membranes. We excrete through orifices.

How uniform the shape and stink of our similar shit as well as the froth of our piss-foam in a urinal or toilet.

I've re-named my era as the United Stages of America. It began one evening while I was smoking my pipe and preparing to give a boy a handful of Halloween candy. He stared at the pipe and said, "What's that?" That was the first of many multi-adjustments I had to make. Next came a wedding where the bride had her wedding date tattooed on the back of her neck. Then came the bishop who denied having abused girls by claiming it was actually only boys. Then cars that could drive, warn, brake to a stop and park themselves. Then trips to the moon for three million dollars round-trip. Then tracing ancestors back to Adam or part way. Then adolescents who were never taught to write cursively and ended by printing their thoughts and messages, which suggested there would be few or no handwritten love letters from them in the future. Then a rare third-grader who said, "Poetry is putting your best words together and putting feeling in them." There's hope.

John Berger: "The moment of truth is now. And more and more it will be poetry, rather than prose, that receives this truth. Prose is far more trusting than poetry; poetry speaks to the immediate wound."

The etymological meaning of Allah is "He who is."

John Keats: "Poetry should surprise by a fine excess and not by singularity—it should strike the reader as a wording of his own thoughts, and appear almost a remembrance."

Told she had perfect breasts, she smiled and said, "True for now, but we know what happens to them."

Of the 3,419,000,000 people on the earth, 2,324,000,000 live under repressive or dictatorial governments. This means that 1,095,000,000 live under democratically elected governments, and this figure includes India's 5 47,000,000.

Anonymous Egyptian poem, 1000 B.C.

> O my beloved
> how sweet it is
> to go down
> and bathe in the pool
> before your eyes
> letting you see how
> my drenched linen dress
> marries
> the beauty of my body.
> Come, look at me.

Amy Seifreed: "It is often easier for people to give their bodies than it is to give their hearts. Victor Hugo writes in *Les Miserables*—'...young people love with their hearts before they can love with their bodies. Old souls love with their bodies before they love with their hearts, if they can.'"

We have a tendency to villainize our enemies—or rather, over-villainize them.

War-weather.

The thumb is the tongue of the hand.

An adage; "Tell me, I forget. Show me, I remember. Involve me, I understand.

Christa McAuliffe: "I touch the future. I teach."

To paraphrase Emerson, we are who we are before we are inclined to be identified by what we do, which means that the priorities of being in the order of nature precede the priorities of doing.

Emerson writes of intuition (what comes from spontaneity and instinct) and tuition (what comes from instruction or tutelage). Intuition is the act of knowing without the usual rational processes. It is what qualifies as insight—an immediate and undeniable cognition. Tuition or tutelage is learned by doing and is allied with instruction. Intuition is related to inspiration.

An adage: "Lose parents, and you lose the past. Lose children, and you lose the future. Lose your mate, and you lose the present."

The use of body deodorant is related to a fear of rejection by the tribe. The underlying prod is "Even your best friends won't tell you."

Bill McCleary said that in every great story or play the leading character must be motivated by some hunger. Odysseus hungered to return home to Ithaca after twenty years of war and exile. Hamlet hungered for justice to avenge the murder of his father. Romeo and Juliet hungered for one another. For the old fisherman in Hemingway's *The Old Man and the Sea* the hunger was for catching the ultimate fish. But the main character's hunger must be accompanied by a plan to satisfy it. That's what constitutes the story—hunger and a plan,

Emily Grosholz in *The Gold Earrings:* "Not that memory grows less intense, but the period of recollection lengthens."

The Israeli government has threatened to arrest Hannan Ashrawi, a prominent Palestinian intellectual and member of the PLO. They have charged her with contact with the PLO, which she openly has admitted. The interesting footnote to this is that the Israelis consider her "dangerously articulate."

A French adage: *"Les gens heureux n'ont pas d'histoire."*

John Ruskin: "The greatest thing a human soul ever does in this world is to see something, and tell what it saw in a plain way. Hundreds of people can talk for one who can think, but thousands can think for one who can see. To see clearly is poetry, prophecy and religion all in one."

82% of the population of India cannot read or write, making it a listening population. Seven out of ten high school students in New York own or have access to guns. 8% of black children come from single-parent families. There are 80 homicides per day in the United States contrasted with 13 in England, 26 in Canada and 47 in Japan. 35% of the population of Philadelphia is functionally illiterate.

Bartlett Giamatti: "No good teacher ever wants to control the contour of another's mind. That would not be teaching; it would be a form of terrorism."

She sat in waiting at attention. Scheduled to be doctored in, doctored through and doctored out, we all were waiting to be told, "The doctor will see you now." Some fingered their cell phones or read outdated waiting room copies of *Time* or *People* or did their best to look unhappy. Upright and calm, she was the lone exception. Leaving, I paused and asked her, "Excuse me, but can you take a compliment?" She looked surprised and said, "What's the reason for the compliment?" I referred to her erect posture in the waiting room. She smiled and added, "My mother said that sitting tall is nothing more than standing tall when you're sitting down."

Evil is said to begin with the intention. This means that one succumbs to evil as a thought or plan whether the evil as contemplated becomes a fact or not. But conceiving of good or planning to do good is without intrinsic merit unless it ensues in action. This means that goodness is not really goodness unless it is translated into action. Evil on the other hand exists from the moment it exists as a thought.

Which is superior—to inform or to inspire? Put another way...is information more valuable than inspiration?

Albert Camus wrote that the central problem of our century is the legalizing of murder, i.e., legalized killing. He cites war and capital punishment as the prime examples. I would say that abortion and, where legalized, euthanasia are also examples of legal murder since lives are taken in both instances by other human beings. All of these killings involve the taking of innocent lives, and law is used as a justification in the same way it is used to justify war and executions.

One man described the Russian Revolution as the greatest event in human history, saying that what happened in November of 1917 had no peer in history. Another man then asked him, "One thousand nine hundred and seventeen years after what?"

Ben al-Hamara, an Arab poet of Andalusia, commented on insomnia: "When the bird of sleep thought to nest in my pupils, it saw the lashes and fled in fear of the net."

Jerzy Kosinski, from *Passing By:* "It took Napoleon to figure out that with the cubic content of just one Great Pyramid one could fence France with a barrier one foot wide and ten feet high—an achievement not even his Napoleonic brain could conceive of."

The rooster may crow, but the hen delivers.

Melissa DeSimone, a student: "Memories will be of the chances taken and the lessons learned, both good and bad, not of the opportunities missed."

Poverty unites; prosperity divides.

The Caesar salad was concocted by two Italian brothers named Cardini in Tijuana in the 1920's. It's a perfect example of how an obscure concoction or discovery could gradually become known throughout the world, presumably without advertising, because it was good and people liked it and said so. Isn't this also true of poems, which are written in obscurity, sometimes even suppressed, but survive nonetheless and become known by millions over the centuries because they spoke and speak and continue to speak to everybody always everywhere?

Can it be said that those who believe in abortion—on demand or otherwise—are really making an unadmitted defense of parental irresponsibility?

During the Middle Ages certain Christians, believing in stereotypical and prejudiced prototypes of Jews, literally conceded doctoring and financing to Jews because they thought the body and money were evil and did not want to be contaminated.

Stephen Dunn in *Walking Light:* "Robert Frost wrote that 'grievances are a form of impatience,' and went on to say that he didn't like them in poetry. He preferred 'griefs.' Yeats told us that quarrels produce rhetoric. Poetry comes out of quarrels with oneself."

Cardinal John Henry Newman: "In the nature of things, greatness and unity come together; excellence implies a center."

A third grader: "The room was so big I felt rich."

Chinese fortune cookie: "Discontent is the beginning of change in the life of a nation."

Yannis Ritsos: "Death is always there, but it comes second. Freedom comes first."

The free marketeer is in a sense the total counterpart of the ultimate communist. Where the communist would have state control of consumers' and producers' goods (supplies and the sources of supplies), the free marketeer would defy control over anything, i.e. *laissez faire* and *caveat emptor*. The assumption in both cases is that the system will solve the problem. Both are wrong for different reasons, of course, because, at bottom, systems must be made for man, not man for the systems. The system must always be meant to accommodate human needs.

"We are all mortal until the first kiss and the second glass."

Helen Bevington (at eighty-six): "I'm treated with unbearable respect and occasional alarm for remaining upright."

Victories are rarely solutions, but most genuine solutions are true victories.

The Greeks of the classical age understood that tragedies were invariably domestic, i.e., Oedipus and his family, Medea and her braggart of a husband etc. Homer based the *Iliad* on the fact that a war was waged because one man made off with another man's wife. And the *Odyssey* is essentially a story of a man's struggle to reach home and family. Shakespeare wrote thematically in the same tradition; his best tragedies arise out of domestic situations, i.e., a girl and a boy who love one another despite the traditional enmities of their families, a college student whose uncle, the murderer of his father, is now married to his mother and who is admonished to act, an old man's treatment at the hands of his daughter. Domestic tragedies, all of them....

Jacket copy for Seamus Heaney's play: "*The Cure at Troy* dramatizes the conflict between personal integrity and political expediency, and it further explores ways in which the victims of injustice can become as devoted to the contemplation of their wounds as the perpetrators are to the justification of their system."

I remember that it was Etienne Gilson who said that the act of faith requires a "leap." In other words, one does not believe because knowledge leads one to do so. It is not knowledge that underlies the sudden possibility of belief. On the contrary, one believes because one reaches a point beyond which knowledge does not nor cannot take us. At that point one "leaps." Any knowledge that comes as a result of one's believing from having taken the "leap" of faith —of believing *first*—is the direct result of that original act. Any knowledge that is gained from study or in any other way that gives an intellectual character to belief is, in Gilson's words, "a positive gain to the understanding."

La Rochefoucauld: "Absence will make a strong passion stronger and a weak one weaker."

Nietzsche's definition of an unhappy man is "one whose future is behind him and whose past is ahead of him."

Gertrude Stein: "An American wife may rise to the occasion in a crisis, but a French wife thinks it wise to keep the crisis from arising."

Robert Frost to Sidney Cox: "To be too subjective about what an artist has managed to make objective is to come on him presumptuously and render ungraceful what he in pain of his life had faith he made graceful."

To the Africans their head-dresses were homage to the "sacredness of the head." These same people painted their bodies so that they would be "distinguished from animals."

Samuel Hynes in *The Soldier's Tale* says that in the First World War (and probably all wars) soldiers on line simply regarded cowardice as "fear at its most extreme." He also praises a "brave fight for a lost cause" and adds that "Hell is a place without why."

Heraclitus: "We share a world when we are awake; each sleeper is in a world of his own....Awake, we see a dying world; asleep, dreams."

A barber never lets his scissors stop talking.

I'm driving behind a horse trailer with a horse aboard, it black tail brooming the latched gate, swish by swish.

Anwar Sadat bought pre-owned Dunhill pipes in George-town when he came to the United States.

Tomas Elroy Martinez in *Santa Evita:* "He had the bewil-dered expression of someone who has lost himself and doesn't know where to start looking."

The ideal situation for the free enterpriser or free trader is when he can create the supply to meet the demand cre-ated by his own propaganda and advertising. (It was the poet William Matthews who said that "Advertising is the poetry of capitalism.") If the free enterpriser or trader controls or owns the media in which his propaganda and advertising appears, he has an unobstructed road directly to the consumer-to-be. No wonder free traders cry "Foul!" whenever government comes between them and their customers. They prefer to play with the public with no in-tervention.

Consider the difference between crime and sin. Crime is any act or thought that violates the law. Sin is any act that violates the laws of God. Sin is, therefore, a much broader concept than crime. Sexual intercourse between consenting adults outside of marriage in the Judeo-Christian code may not be a crime, but it is a sin. Mutual consent does not make the act sinless even though it may not be punishable by law. In our age we tend to reduce many social evils to the level of a lawless act or crime. Then we attempt to deal with them by making them punishable. Thus, the ideal lawbreaker in the eyes of the lawless is he who can get around the law, i.e. someone who is never caught and tried and punished. In short, the ideal lawbreaker is he who can "get away with it." The sinner, on the other hand, is punished by his own conscience for his sin (which has been identified as the voice of God within him) whether it is a crime or not. You can get away from a crime. You cannot get away from a sin because you, the sinner, are the punisher.

Blanchisserie is the word for a laundry in French. Since the word for "white" in French is "*blanche*," then a laundry is a place of whitening.

Tasso Katselas: "For the Greeks, religion was a game that the gods played with mortals. Later Christian zeal changed into superstition. Still later it turned into a business."

The concise poem of a Volkswagen compared with the blunt prose of a truck...

It's not a question of how long you'd like to live but who you'd like to live long with.

Saving money by availing yourself of sale or bargains is nothing but reverse greed glamorized as prudence or fiscal discipline.

Jefferson bought the Louisiana Purchase from Napoleon for $15,000,000 or close to three cents an acre.

There are such things as bankable pleasures or experiences that a person enjoys and can enjoy repetitively. My little dog seems to know this instinctively. He likes cream cheese and knows—just by seeing it—that it will taste the same when he eats it as it did the last time he ate it. Likewise, there is a small circle of sunlight on the rug near the rear window of our house in the morning, and he lies in that circle every morning because he seems to like the feel of the warm rug under him and the rug-like swath of sun across his body. These are for him bankable pleasures. He can rely on them for satisfaction, and they never fail to satisfy him. So should it be for us. Instead of being titillated by an infinite sophistication of pleasures (better vacations, better cigars, better steaks), why not focus on a few tested pleasures which have held up and which we can rely on to continue to hold up? Take my smoking pipe, for example. I know that it will offer the same pleasure to my taste (and even to my palm when I cradle my pipe in it) time and again. Once when there was a fire alarm in the Vista International Hotel in Washington, I walked down twenty-one floors, and the only thing I brought with me was my pipe.

It is my experience with the French that they make s poof-poof dismissal sound or else a slight clicking of the lips (accompanied by a look of total disapproval and distaste) when they confront something that is demonstrably incorrect or simply absurd.

Shakespeare: "For I must go where lazy Peace will hide her drowsy head: and, for the sport of kings, increase the number of the dead."

Beethoven: "The world's a king, and, like a king, desires flattery in return for favor."

St. John Perse: "A poet is the guilty conscience of his time."

Mario Vargas Llosa: "A writer is...the eternal killjoy."

Vegetarian. Fruiteterian? Fruiterian?

Fundamentalism, particularly in Christianity, is actually an enemy of life. I think of medieval Christians (and some current evangelicals) waiting like zombies for the second coming of Christ. Just waiting. Meanwhile the earth and things of this earth are ignored. Because banking and medicine and music, which were considered "of the flesh" and frivolous, they were left to the Jews and unbelievers, and these groups eventually and predictably began to dominate these professions. Still later, nefarious "Christians" began to indulge in usury. Usury, once condemned as a sin, eventually became legitimized as the profit motive, which is extolled as an incentive today. Techniques of medical science evolved from seeing suffering as a time of spiritual purgation or part of the punishment for original sin to confronting it as a negative condition that medical science existed to cure or relieve. And music went from monody to polyphonics, i.e. from unanimity of tone to tonal variety so that the full spectrum of human feelings could be translated into melody. Fundamentalists ignore these advances in preference a kind of rigor mortis of belief, forgetting that cures are to be sought, crimes solved, charlatans exposed, etc.

James Salter in *The Hunters:* "On a warm day, and all alone, it was not easy to die. Death could be slighted or even ignored close by; but when the time came to meet it unexpectedly, no man could find it in himself not to cry silently or aloud for just one more reprieve to keep the world from ending."

To leave no trace like an "oar's swirl." The phrase is from James Salter.

A poet or any imaginative writer must try to reveal when he writes not just the experience but the "feel" of the experience through his words. He cannot editorialize, which is like moralizing. He must let the meaning assert itself through description without actually saying what it is in other terms. Only the imagination can do that.

Sam of his mother: "Mom is a tough lover."

Rudyard Kipling: "When your demon is in charge, do not try to think consciously. Drift, wait and obey."

Albert Camus: "Mental chastity—prevent your desires from straying, your thoughts from wandering."

Montesquieu: "Europe will be lost by its military men."

E. M. Forster: "The work of art is the only material object in the universe which may possess internal harmony. All the others have been pressed into shape from outside, and when their mold is removed, they collapse. The work of art stands up by itself, and nothing else does. It achieves something which has often been promised by society, but always delusively."

Schopenhauer: "Courage is merely the virtue of a second lieutenant."

Albert Camus: "There is always a philosophy for lack of courage." "Those who write obscurely have great luck. They will have commentators. The others will have only readers, and this, it seems, is worthy of scorn."

John Keats: "There is no greater Sin after the seven deadly than to flatter oneself into an idea of being a great Poet."

Norman Mailer, writing of Mobutu in *The Fight:* "The first rule of dictatorships is to re-enforce your mistakes."

Written of Lou Salome: "She thought with her heart and felt with her head."

Renata Adler in *Gone:* "In technology, you can have customers, a need, investors before the desired product is invented. Trying to create or adapt a product to a market, in other words, makes sense if the product is dishwashers or military hardware. In cultural matters it does not make sense."

Exchanges between Herbert Read and Edward Dahlberg in *Truth Is More Sacred.* Dahlberg: "The misuse of words induces evil in the soul." Read (Speaking of *Lady Chatterly's Lover*): "Mellors, the erotic gamekeeper, Pan in corduroy trousers, a goat with a shotgun." Dahlberg: "Swift created the Lilliputian to show the littleness of man, but he gave us Gulliver to indicate the epic dimensions of humanity." Read: "It is the method of Charity, said Sir Thomas Browne, to suffer without reaction; it is the method of the great poet to write in the sure knowledge that a bright image never loses its luster, though it be buried in the garbage of a doomed civilization."

Montaigne: "She who refuses only because consent is not permitted—consents."

Edward Dahlberg: "Who does not grieve when the summer of his flesh has passed?"

John Bayley: '....the inevitable solace that right language brings."

Shirley Hazzard (of Graham Greene): "Following his death, he became for a while something of a target for the strictures of the righteous: a prey of a spectacle, recently renascent, of virtue addressing error."

The American dollar sign ($) is said to be derived from a warning (S) left by Hercules at Gibraltar—*non plus ultra.*

Of nudism: "Everything displayed (shown); nothing revealed (known)."

Men look; women notice. Men buy; women shop. Men choose; women consider.

Arthur Schlesinger (from *A Life in the Twentieth Century*): He says that his father's "commitment as a scholar" did not abrogate his "conscience as a citizen." In other words, one's work in life is not full citizenship. He adds that society has been taken over by "fundamentalist, super patriots and large corporations"—resulting in "much political freedom" but "so little intellectual and spiritual freedom." He refers to John Henry Newman's *Grammar of Assent*, distinguishing between national assent, which he calls an assent to abstractions, as opposed to real assent, which is an assent to things. He notes that national assent does not affect conduct nor lead to action, but real assent does.

Simone de Beauvoir: "Sartre is persuaded that...modern painting is without a subject, music without a melody, physics without matter. I think he could have added that much modern poetry is without passion or vision as modern life is without purpose or meaning."

William Blake: "For a man to get enthusiastic, things have to happen, while for a woman, things just have to be." "In seed time, learn, in harvest, teach, in winter, enjoy."

Shakespeare (in *King John*): "Grief fills the room up of my absent child, lies in his bed, walks up and down with me, puts on his pretty looks, repeats his words, remembers me of all his gracious parts, stuffs out his vacant garments with his form...Then I have reason to be fond of Grief."

Maybe C. P. Snow had the answer when he said that Cambridge dons are not distinguished men, but merely men who confer distinctions on one another.

Louis Simpson: "Derrida and de Man taught that there was nothing 'beyond language,' no truth— everything was a game played with words. This appealed to American academics who lead sheltered lives. Besides, the kind of people in the States who gravitated to the humanities had only a smattering of learning and were impressed by Europeans who had read Latin and Greek."

Wislawa Szymborska: "...the book of events is always open halfway through." "...the possessive nostalgia of grief."

Tom Meschery's phrase in a poem is likened to Bill Bradley's "muscle memory."

I would say that the biggest social danger that now exists is not that people do not think but that they tend to think in the same way. Who was it who said that the dominating thoughts of the time are those of the ruling class? I assume that this can be pluralized into "ruling classes" without weakening the impact of the statement. Uniformity of thought is the enemy of criticism, and criticism is the essence of dissent, and dissent (as well as the controversy it inevitably creates) is to me the very stuff of public life. This has always meant to me that dissenters should be listened to quite carefully since it requires courage in this day and age to be a dissenter. I do not say that we should heed it just because it is dissent. But it must be carefully respected and heard because of what it means to society. Truth is rarely if ever the exclusive property of the majority—nor of the minority, for that matter. It is not reserved for factions.

The etymology of the word "idiot" in Greek means "he who does not participate in public life."

Carlos Fuentes in *Inez:* "A woman knows more about life, and sooner, than a man, who is slow to give up his childhood. Perpetual adolescent or, worse, aged child. There are few immature women, but many children disguised as men."

Hanning Boetius in *The Phoenix:* "He was the first to determine that if you multiply the volume of a specific gas by its pressure, the product always remains constant. In other words, whenever you reduce the volume, you increase the pressure."

Ian Littlewood in *Sultry Climates:* "Freud asserted that civilization was paid for by the repression and sublimation of the sexual urge." "The prostitute's sphere, like the tourist's, is the world of pleasure as opposed to the world of work, and in her dedication to pleasure she is linked, as the social historian Alain Corbin has argued, with the child and the savage."

Gustave Flaubert: "Whereas the truth is that fullness of soul that can sometimes overflow in utter vapidity of language, for none of us can ever expresses the exact measure of his needs or his thoughts or his sorrows; and human speech is like a cracked kettle on which we tap crude rhythms for bears to dance to, while we long to make music that will melt the stars."

Forty percent of college students in the United States do not take courses in history, and seventy percent do not study a foreign language.

Safari is derived from an Arabic word that means to travel on foot. Safari is Swahili. *Sahafi*, a similar Arabic word, means reporter.

Lucubrate means to write in a scholarly fashion, i.e. pedantic writing, laborious writing.

Michelle Cliff: "The swear word *bloody* is a contraction of 'by my lady', which refers directly to the Virgin Mary."

Carlos Fuentes: "Rhetoric, said William Butler Yeats, is the language of our fight with others; poetry is the name of our fight with ourselves."

Arthur Miller in *The Bare Manuscript:* "His view was that a man had to go somewhere with his erection, while a woman felt that she was somewhere. A big difference."

Catholics are purportedly less prone to suicide than Protestants, but more prone to murder.

Consider Victor Hugo's, "In Paris they argue. In Avignon they kill."

Perfervid=passionate. Gravid=pregnant.

Patti Pope: "My brother is so good he's boring."

A female character in a novel explains her infidelity to her husband by saying frankly, "I was just tired of being good."

Romano Guardini: "The soul must learn to abandon, at least in prayer, the restlessness of purposeful activity; it must learn to waste time for the sake of God."

H. L. Mencken: "...puritanism....the haunting fear that someone, somewhere, may be happy. "

Harold Bodkey: "Reading is an intimate act, perhaps more intimate than any act. I say this because of the prolonged (or intense) exposure of one mind to another."

Virginia Woolf: "At the heart of the pleasure of reading is the delight of a free union, like a very intimate conversation or an act of love."

Michael Haullebecq: "Not having anything around to read is dangerous: you have to content yourself with life itself, and that can lead you to take risks."

Quote from Anna Hazo: "Yes, I'm not." "That's what we don't." "I want to tell you a speakret." "Hang it down (as opposed to hang it up)." "Baby genius," (Said of Jesus in the crib). "Scale me." (Weigh me).

Robert Frost from "Snow": "Things must expect to come in front of us/A many time—I don't say just how many—/That varies with the tings—before we see them./One of the lies would make it out that nothing/Evil presents itself before us twice./Where would we be at last if that were so./Our very life depends on everything's/Recurring till we answer from within./The thousandth time may prove the charm."

J. M. Coetzee (spoken by one of the characters in *Elizabeth Costello:* "When we Africans visit great European cities like Paris or London, we notice how people on trains take books out of their bags or their pocket and retreat into solitary worlds. Each time the book comes out is like a sign held up. Leave me alone. I am reading, says the sign. What I am reading is more interesting than you could possibly be."

Eduardo Galeano: "The powerful who legitimize their privileges by heredity cultivate nostalgia."

Noam Chomsky: "What remains of democracy is largely the right to choose among commodities. Business leaders have long explained the need to impose on the population a philosophy of futility and a 'lack of purpose in life,' to concentrate on human attention on the more superficial things that comprise much of fashionable consumption. Deluged by such propaganda from infancy, people may accept their meaningless and subordinate lives and forget ridiculous ideas about managing their own affairs. They may abandon their fate to corporate managers and the PR industry and, in the political realm, to the self-descried 'intelligent minorities' who serve and administer power."

Mavis Gallant: "The distinction between journalism and fiction is the difference between without and within. Journalism recounts as exactly and economically as possible the weather in the street; fiction takes no notice of the particular weather but brings to life a distillation of all weathers, a climate of the mind. Which is not say it need not be exact and economical; it is a precision of a different order."

Shakespeare (from *Hamlet*):

> *Hamlet:* No, not I. I never gave you aught.
> *Ophelia:* My honor'd lord, you know right well
>   you did
> And with them words of so sweet breath
>   compos'd
> As made these things more rich. Their perfume
>   lost,
> Take these again, for to the noble mind
> Rich gifts wax poor when givers prove unkind.
> There, my lord...
> *Hamlet (eleven lines later):* Where's your father?
> *Ophelia:* He is without, my lord.

For me this is the lowest point in the play for Hamlet since he knows that Polonius is in hiding and listening to the conversation. It is when Ophelia, the only person he thinks he can trust, lies to him that Hamlet's unraveling begins.

Alan Richardson (from *The Nation*): "I have come to the conclusion that conservatives look for the ideal society in the past, whereas liberals look to the future. Progress then is a liberal idea whereas the good old days are conservative. Neocons, however, look to their egregiously erroneous view of the future."

Anna: "Where did Oscar go?" (Oscar was our dog. He had just died.) Poppo (me): "Oscar went to heaven." Anna: "When is he coming back?" Poppo:: "Well, when you go to heaven, you don't come back. Oscar won't be coming back." Anna: "Is he in jail in heaven?" Poppo:: "No, but he won't be coming back." Anna: "It's okay, Poppo, be happy."

Gurt Mak (from *In Europe*): "Hitler's optimistic assault on the Soviet Union, and above all his declaration of wars on the United States, belong in that row of historical errors precipitated by groupthink: doctrines made by small groups of policy-makers who see themselves as all-powerful, and who dismiss all problems by refusing to admit any undesirable information from outside. Leaders—great and small—the phenomenon has been seen at all levels and in every age—can in this way create for themselves a fictitious world that will sooner or later, but inevitably, come crashing down"

William Pfaff: "The idea of total and redemptive transformation through political means, the most influential myth of modern Western political society from 1789 to the present day, remains with us. It has been discredited only in its Marxist and Fascist versions, which far from exhaust its present and future possibilities. Its naïve American version, though hardly recognized as such, survives, consisting in the belief that generalizing American-style political institutions and economic practices in the world at large will bring history (or at least historical progress) to its present fulfillment."

J. M. Coetzee (spoken by one of the characters in *Elizabeth Costello*): "When we Africans visit great European cities like Paris or London, we notice how people on trains take books out of their bags or their pocket and retreat into solitary worlds. Each time the book comes out is like a sign held up. Leave me alone. I am reading, says the sign. What I am reading is more interesting than you could possibly be."

My brother Bob told me once that you can never underestimate the gullibility of the American electorate. I can think of two instances in the last century that support my brother's insight. The first was the 1972 election of Richard Nixon for a second term. To me Nixon was the same superficial and callow man that I saw in person in Norfolk, Virginia, when he was running with Dwight Eisenhower in 1952. He had the same speech patterns, the same habit of raising his hands in a phony V, the same smile that was not quite a smile. On the other hand he was vying with George McGovern, who was an obviously good man if you consider a man good when his words reflect his actual feeling and thoughts, who was an Air Force veteran with multiple missions over Japan on his record, who was an experienced senator as well as a holder of a doctorate in history. Paired with McGovern as the Vice-Presidential nominee was Sergeant Shriver, the original top official when the Peace Corps was created in the Kennedy administration. The result was that Nixon won every state but Massachusetts and the District of Columbia. Amazing! That may never be topped. Three years later Nixon resigned to avoid a criminal trial.

A second example revealing the gullibility of the electorate happened during the Reagan administration. Never an admirer of Reagan, I nonetheless could never work up a total disregard for the man. He fulfilled role of President acceptably with regard to exteriors; he was handsome, he wore a suit well, and he did not seem vindictive by nature. I simply found him corny. When the Iran scandal broke and Reagan retreated into amnesia, I happened to be in France. I watched the Senate hearings during which a certain Marine Corps colonel was called to testify. His name was Oliver North. Looking boyishly military, he took the oath to tell the truth, the whole truth and nothing but the truth and then proceeded to paint a hyper-patriotic version of what Iran-Contra involved that was totally at odds with the facts as they were known at the time. He did this under oath and in uniform before a Senate committee. Hiding crimes behind symbols of patriotism is an old Washington story, and I made up my mind then and there that North fitted the script precisely. When I returned to the United States, I found myself to be in the barely visible minority that had a similar view of North. I heard him praised for everything from his haircut to what he did for his country in the name of a higher patriotism. In short, he was regarded by a majority of Americans as a complete patriot—a Marine's Marine. North was eventually pardoned and subsequently ran for a Senate seat—the same Senate he had previously mocked with false testimony—and lost. He eventually became an evangelical celebrity of sorts on extended lecture tours and finally the host of a television program extolling military heroism.

Luftwaffe means air weapon.

Anatole France: "To know is nothing; to imagine is everything." Author unknown: "Knowing is stifling; not knowing is creative."

Sarah (at twelve): "You should never tell a woman to calm down."

At military cemeteries the visitors rarely come in crowds. Those who are the relatives of the dead—the traditional next of kin—often bring fresh flowers to put on the grave. They remaining standing in contemplation, remembrance or prayer, talk briefly, then leave, each in the sacred chapel of his or her own memories. Soldiers visiting the graves of their fallen comrades-in-arms are only slightly different. They come as if summoned by voices they once knew well. They walk carefully between the ordered aisles of crosses (with here and there a Star of David), and they search for names on the white cross-arms. When they find a name they recognize, they stop. They are quiet for some time. The bite their lips, shake their heads slowly, shift from foot to foot, walk away with a sense of weariness. Sometimes they return to repeat the ritual. They are chewing the bitter bread of survival, wondering for what reason or by what act of God or fate they still walk the earth while others whom they knew are now buried in it. They stare at the dates below the names and ranks on the cross or markers. Each date is when a life stopped or rather when the living of that life was stopped. But somehow the life itself did not stop but went more mysteriously on, burying the years that followed, burying the decades, burying a quarter of a century so that kin or comrades returning to graves are confronted by an eternal present, a time that will never be (can never be) clocked or calendared. The dead, the unkillable dead remain invisibly there with a certainty that is undeniable. That is finally the mystery of death—the mystery of the stopped but unstoppable life. I remember the title of a story I read years ago entitled "In the Midst of Death We Live." I've long since forgotten the story, but I'll never forget the title because it is the permanent address of all of us.

I knew for months that he was dying, but somehow I could not bring myself to visit him. Having known him from our days in high school, I did not have the courage to face a man of fifty who was dying of cancer. Finally, more out of impulse or guilt, I called his wife—whom I knew better than I knew him—and asked if I could pay a visit. She suggested that I come the following afternoon. Twenty-four hours later I rang the doorbell of their home and waited. When she opened the door and welcomed me, I noticed that she looked wan. Not weak or morose, but wan. The strength was there, but so was the strain. We talked for a time about various things, and she seemed in no hurry to let me see her husband. She did tell me several times that he was heavily sedated, but that I should still try to talk to him when I saw him. Some words, she said, would get through. Still, she seemed in no hurry to initiate the visit, and I realized much, much later that she was delaying so as to prepare me for what I would see. Actually, what could have prepared me to see a man who probably weighed less than a hundred pounds supine in maroon pajamas on a sheeted bed on which there were no pillows or blankets? A nurse was sitting beside the bed. She stood up when I entered. After a brief conversation between her and my friend's wife, she lifted the man as if he weighed no more than a towel and seated him gently in the cushioned chair she had just vacated. She then edged a second chair close to the cushioned chair and gestured for me to sit down. Meanwhile my friend's wife was talking quietly to him, telling him who I was, calling him her darling and easing his hair out of his open but unfocused eyes. Her touch was the touch of a lover, so gentle and familiar that it could have been her own hair that she was re-arranging. Then she kissed him, put one of his limp hands in mine and left the room with the nurse. After a pause I began to talk, but I scarcely remember what I said. His head drooped forward, and his eyes still had the comatose glaze of someone unconscious or too heavily drugged to be aware of anything around him. His hand in mine was as light as the paw of a cat. I could not forget how his wife had talked to him moments before, how she looked at him, how she lifted his hair and stroked his forehead and then kissed him. She was not in the presence of a sick and dying man when she did that (in fact he died the following day) but in the presence of the man she loved, sickness and death notwithstanding.

A Japanese maple over a single summer exhibits a chromatic scale of color. What begins as the color of port wine gradually changes to maroon and then to greenish-maroon and then in autumn to light brown and finally to tan. I have never seen any other tree transform itself that way.

The dogs and sparrows were moving up a one-way street the wrong way. It made the street seem wrong.

Cemeteries around country churches are as orderly as the parked cars in the parking lots next to the churches.

If now is never long enough for lovers, what is it for the rest of us?

When Orpheus sings, the whole world stops.

We keep ignoring Emerson's observation that we are men before we are teachers, pilots, presidents or anything else. If we try to submerge ourselves totally in our work or even go as far as to identify ourselves with what we do as if all else does not exist, it can take something as minuscule as a pebble in our shoe or the nuisance of a cold to remind us of our mortal natures. And the final reminder is death itself. We don't die as writers, lawyers or engineers. We die as men.

When I'm asked if I'm a liberal or a conservative, traditional or radical, a revolutionist or an evolutionist, I pause. There is something doctrinaire in such questions, and I will never commit myself to any question that commits me to an answer any more than I will commit myself to a solution before I know the problem. If this implies that I might have to contradict myself in the process, then I say with Whitman, "Very well, I contradict myself."

There is no present tense of the verb *to be* in Arabic. When I asked why, I was told that the Arabs, originally a nomadic people, saw time as cyclical rather than linear. Between what had already happened and what would happen, the present was merely a transitional state and somehow unreal. Can this be true?

For some the impulse to obey some person or accede without forethought to a certain order or trend could be a way of evading facing what philosophers call the human condition. Not knowing in advance the month or day of our final year, we often yield to a tendency to let life happen. Actually, knowing these final facts in advance would make life seem like living out a sentence. At these moments we are vulnerable more or less to solutions that supposedly rid us of anxiety. These "solutions" could be religious or psychological or simply wishful thinking, but for us to embrace them—or be obedient to them—could mean that we surrender our capacity for independent thought, and thinking independently is the basis of individual freedom of mind, no matter how onerous the demands of such freedom may be.

Books on shelves are like silent ranks at attention—Shakespeare, Saroyan, Read and Padilla. Each book keeps to itself but seems convivial in proximity with the others. And each one is or used to be but will always be someone. Books come to us with the intent of becoming total friends. We can visit or consult them whenever or wherever we choose, and we read them (even if we've read them before). Our attention brings them to life again and again. They are testaments to the unburiability of life. The dead won't stay dead. They survive in books, in children, in what they've made or done, in memory itself. And they live with us even more intimately in their very absence— their physical absence. Consider James Joyce's short story *The Dead*. A family's annual party has gone on routinely for year after year. All the family members attend, as expected. The aging spinsters, who are the hosts, get older every year, and their voices when they sing their expected solos of old songs sound reedier every year. They sing as they fade. But suddenly the memory evoked by one song brings a moment of utter and undeniable truth to one married couple. The annual dinners will never be the same for them again. The dead, having reappeared through the intervention of an overheard song, have intervened at a time of their choosing and given their silent transforming commands.

I would find it difficult to celebrate Easter in the tropics where the climate and vegetation are more or less the same all year. For me, Easter is associated with Spring, and there seems to be a logical link between the feast of the Resurrection and the reappearance of green after the long hibernation of the cold months. The fact that nature is really unkillable and that vegetation renews itself annually seems like a perfect counterpart for the spirit's triumph over death, which is very essence of Christianity itself and what is central to the feast of Easter.

In his *Sonnets To Orpheus* Rainer Maria Rilke states that only those who have sojourned for a time to hell and returned have earned the right to sing of joy. "Only whoso has raised/among the shades his lyre/dares, with foreboding, aspire/to offer infinite praise./No one but that one/who has eaten with the dead/their poppies will never forget/the softest tone./Though the picture in the pool/ before s grows dim:/Make the image yours./Only in the dual/Realm will voices become eternal and pure." This preamble of suffering before a joyful epiphany is common enough in all human experience, but Orpheus infuses it with love. Indeed love—the love of Orpheus for Eurydice —- is the very reason Orpheus went to hell and sang persuasively enough before Pluto that Pluto returned her to Orpheus. Suppose, in less mystical terms, that a modern Orpheus, mourning his dead wife, descended into hell where she alone remained alive for him. Would his sojourn there, like that of Orpheus into hell itself, so qualify him to sing joyfully when his memory released him to the present tense again?

It was Leon Bloy who said that there are places in the heart that actually do not exist until suffering creates them. This means that the heart is forever being enlarged or re-created since suffering of one kind or another is a constant part of human life. I know from my own experience how painful such enlargements can be, and I can truthfully say that I never accepted any painful experiences gracefully that resulted in such spaces in the heart. In fact, in every instance I resisted what was happening to me. In fact, in every instance I resisted, never accepting until reality itself left me no choice. What is ironic is that inevitably a burst of creative energy followed such struggles. A number of years ago I fractured my leg in three places, and my lack of mobility while the bones were knitting made me introspective to such a point that I began chronicling my introspections into what turned into an entire book. Most of it dealt with memories of my life in Pittsburgh. Had it not been for that fracture—fortuitous in retrospect—I doubt seriously I would ever have undertaken to write such a narrative. Similarly, many of the poems I have written seem like reactions to some reversal or shock. In every instance I can say that these are examples of some of the best writing of which I think I am capable, but I can also say that in every case I wish I had never had reasons to write them. I suppose I can say that these writings were a kind of salvation, a way of coming of coming to terms with whatever it was that had wounded me, of objectifying an inwardness into something that had a name. Even now I can go back and read those poems or recite them public without feeling the eviscerating pain that prompted them into being, which is life's gratuitous anesthetic against past sorrows Sometimes they make me think that they were written by someone else or that they wrote themselves.

Knowledge without imagination is inert. It is imagination that makes knowledge the basis for creative thought or action. It is imagination that relates one aspect of knowledge to another and seeks their integration. But it is also the imagination that holds the knower to account. Consider the ongoing issues relative to racism in the United States. It is one thing to know that that anything that compromises the constitutional assurance of the self-evident equality of all men is contrary to the proclamations of the Constitution. Knowing that did not and has not prevented numerous violations in American history. In 1847 there was a growing fear that Mexico might be included in the United States. John Calhoun of North Carolina vigorously opposed this in undisguisedly racist terms: "We have never dreamt of incorporating into our Union any but the Caucasian race—the free white race. Ours is the government of the white man." The strain of white supremacy persists in our social life to this day even though the ideal of equality of all citizens regardless of race, creed or color has been and is guaranteed in and by the Constitution. In other words, race is not relevant to citizenship, constitutionally speaking. But this constitutional ideal of equality as imagined and stated by the founders continues to be subverted by the visceral demands of racists, tribalists or others. Perhaps it was his sensitivity to this that led Alexis de Toqueville to say: "Race will always be a problem in America." This demonstrates that it is one thing to know the Constitution of the United States, and it is the failure of its acceptance by certain citizens that explains the difference between knowledge and action. Knowing and seeing that Constitutional guarantees prevail is a challenge to the imagination. Only the imagination is capable of facilitating the translation of Constitutional truths to pubic life.

Becoming an old man does not mean becoming old as a man. There is a difference. The actuarial and the actual are not synonymous and are rarely on speaking terms with one another. There are men who are old men at thirty while others seem young at seventy. This distinction can only be made by defining what is meant by "old" and "young." Being young usually is understood to mean being at the fullness of one's powers. It implies good health, firmness of mind and so forth. Being old usually means one is past the fullness of one's powers and is no longer equal to meeting challenges that he could have met with impunity when younger. As working definitions, these two would seem to define the differences between youth and age. But they do not explain the way that certain young people seem old while some older people seem young. Is it a matter of spirit, after all, and not a matter of those physical capabilities that naturally weaken or are otherwise diminished as a person grows older? Certainly, losing one's capacity to hear well or to see distinctly or to kneel and rise without pain are not conditions that anyone would see as conditions to celebrate. Nor would it be anything but dispiriting to find oneself unequal to doing what one once could do quite well. For substantiation just look at the unconcealable sadness of professional athletes when they are forced to retire from a sport at which they excelled. Perhaps the real sadness of age occurs when one faces and accepts the fact that life by nature proceeds to a lessening of capabilities (or even a degeneration) as the years mount. Some people accept while others are saddened by the realization that the game of life is essentially a game of loss. Others seem to live at their fullest, moment by moment, and turn their eyes away from whatever appears to be their ultimate end by focusing on the present. It seems to me that non-acceptance (or outright refusal) is key to maintaining a sense of youth in life after the very juices of life have begun to harden.

Absurdity is the essence of baseball. What follows I've said before, but it bears repeating. The initial irony is that the defense has the ball. If the pitcher does not pitch, the game never starts. And even when he does pitch, he does his best to keep the hitter from hitting the ball. (The ultimate irony is that the perfect game—where there are no hits—is when nothing happens.) Even if the batter does get his bat on the ball—the hitting of a ball thrown at speeds of eighty or ninety-plus miles per hour has been described as the most difficult feat in sports—, there are seven fielders plus the pitcher and catcher whose goal is to prevent the batter from reaching first base. The result is that the best batters know in advance that they will approximately seven of ten times. I doubt if there is another game that has a higher rate of failure. All of these are interesting speculations, but the final and most defining characteristic is that the runners round the bases counterclockwise. This further stresses the fact that baseball is not governed by the clock—by hours and minutes. It is a game played under no imposed governance by the clock. It is played in space and is created and governed by actions performed in space until one side or the other in nine innings or more has scored one or more winning runs.

Whenever I miss a stair, my son is there to steady me. We've grown from father to son to something like brother to brother and now like son to father. He knows when I pretend to hear what I never heard even with my healthy ear. Without his mother, I live a life more posthumous than annual. It makes me see obituaries as creative non-fiction, headlines as epitaphs, and war as the price demanded by the curse of wealth. Meanwhile, I do what must be done but find it boring. My calendar has no brakes. Mid-winter is almost past, and already it's the Fourth of July. I cook and brew coffee for one. I read and chew the scrambled prose called news. Each night I dread the torture of nightmares.

I've spent all morning watching chipmunks. They peek nose-first from open-ended tunnels and scoot for a fallen berry. Everything they do they do with ultimate precision even if it means reversing course in a one-way tunnel. No motion is wasted. Turning away, I unfold the morning paper. Hundreds have been gunned to death while dancing in Paris. A drone has targeted a wedding party in Iraq. A scientist warns that New York or Moscow could vanish in a single bombing. The chipmunks chew until they're full while I re-fold the world and watch. And wait.

I learn to write what I'm not sure I know until I write it down. Yesterday's jottings were: "All of us have secrets or shames we never reveal, even to ourselves," and "Men and women hear the same story differently." Hardly original, but that's the way I render visible and verbal, whenever possible, what's visible or invisible. Mary Anne's flowers have all blossomed—a symphony without an overture. Daffodils bloom yellow, cream, orange and gold. Hyacinths unsleeve their pinks and purples. The Japanese cherry's every branch is jammed with buds, multiple buds, hundreds of buds. I swallow a breath and taste each scent of all that color. There are no words.

Imagine Shakespeare or Donne networking for a Renaissance version of a Pulitzer or sucking up to some foundation for a grant. Imagine a workshop of groupies hatching a communal poem and dubbing it their gift to the "poetry scene." Imagine laureates cranking out a poem on demand. If that sounds more like politics than poetry, it should because it *is*. But what of scops and sonneteers from either coast who vie to be the spokesmen for the muse? Or those anointed by anointers self-appointed as the "very voices of our time?" Or poetry readings (why *readings* instead of *hearings?*) where bards of a feather flock together to mimic the bards of yore? Accustomed to the page but not the stage, today's pied pipers tout their anthems for the easily entranced while feminists damn men for damning women to inconsequence, and droners ration out their lines as if they are too sacred to be shared or even heard? Let those who say that poetry is purest when confined to cults, classrooms or cliques sleep on. Let those who say they're poets– as if the *saying* makes it so— be likened to Christians, outspoken and re-born, who make a fool of God by seeing Christ in no one but themselves.

"All I can do is urge you to write without illusions until the words sing off the page. When nouns and verbs make music, something surprising is happening. Wait, wait as long as possible for what's evolving into song so you can be the singer. The words that come may be a mix of yours and others. This means you have a lot of weeding and whittling to do. What you retain will be destined for readers in a future you will never see. Because poems have birthdays but no funerals, they outlive their authors. Any poem you write could have a fate like that, although that's far from certain in advance...After what you hoped to do is done, at least as far being done is possible, you'll find yourself unable to account for or explain exactly how you did it."

What urges them to do it? Swallowing a sword takes practice, and so does walking a tightrope high above Manhattan or braving sharks to swim from Florida to Cuba. Such acts extol defiance, but all for what? Aristotle claimed that courage means doing what's right repeatedly regardless of the odds. All else he called bravado or perversions of the will where reason and imagination fail. Goebbels and Hitler hectored millions to believe that one man's will made thinking by the population as a whole irrelevant. Because the will is vain without the mind, disaster followed. For us the daily firing squads of warfare, illness, crime and accidents remind us of demise. Reactions range from self-pity to self-murder. What else explains why sixteen hundred people have died to date by jumping from the Golden Gate Bridge?

Nobody ever dies but passes. No one has problems but issues. Soldiers are not people but assets. Liars are rarely said to lie but to misspeak. Abortion on demand is never life-ending but a right. When poets say what is *is*, they're seen as dangerous. Dictators burn their books before they jail or murder them. Plato branded poets as dangers to the Republic because they saw the future as present and said so. That leaves no room for rest.

Poems have birthdays but no funerals. They outlive the lives of their creators and the times and cultures in which they were written.

In a different spirit the beatitudes of Christ consecrated the life of man on this planet not as a sentence but as a journey—a journey that ended in a reunion. Paul of Tarsus stated that this journey should be suffused with love: "Yea, though I speak with the tongues of men and angels and have not love, I am become as sounding brass or a tinkling cymbal. And if I should have faith so that I could move mountains and have not love, it profiteth me nothing. And if I should give all my goods to feed the poor and give my body to be burned and have not love, it goes for nothing." Speaking of the need for love during the brevity of our lives, John Donne was prompted to write: "I cannot say I loved./For who can say he was killed yesterday?"

In our own era and our own vernacular Jo McDougall wrote this epitaph about the takeover of a family restaurant by a franchise:

> They put plastic over the menus.
> They told the waitresses to wear white shoes.
> They fired Rita.
> They threw out the unclaimed keys
> and the pelican with a toothpick
> that bowed as you left.

These are but a few examples of poems or poetic passages that persist because they not only cannot be forgotten but because those who remember them derive a unique pleasure in quoting them to others. With literature as with the other arts, time eventually separates the wheat from the chaff. The best expressions endure forever. Shakespeare died at fifty-two, but the language of his poetry and plays have reached millions in multiple countries over six centuries. The same is true of John Keats who lived only long enough to be half as old as Shakespeare when he died. And then there's Robert Frost whose life in decades topped them both but whose poems will outlast his eighty-nine years. But who quotes Nero, Genghis Khan, Benito Mussolini, Adolph Hitler or Senator Joseph Mc-Carthy except in derision of as historical excrescences?

The loss of a dentist, barber or colleague leaves a void without a name. Replacements may be better or worse but never quite as good. How could they be? Perhaps I make too much of it, but loss is loss. The cloth is one and indivisible. I think of Ted with drill and pick in hand but always smiling. Rarely did he "talk teeth" except to say he gave priority to pain. Later I read that aborigines in dental agony would plunge headfirst and screaming onto rocks to end their torment. I thought a lot more gratefully of Ted and dentists after reading that... And there was Ralph who cut my father's hair, my son's, his son's and mine. No one can equal that. Since haircuts mattered as a kind of art for Ralph, we sat enthroned and bibbed for scissors, clippers, talcum and the rest and left renewed and younger... If Al's three loves were students, Shakespeare and Regina, there were no seconds. A scholar in full, he gladly learned and gladly taught. Like Newman's Oxford acolytes whose total creed was "Credo in Newmanum," Al's students swore by Al. And said so. And say so still... Today my life is minus three good men. Accepting that is hard. But seeing in their faces earlier the looming certainty of evening...that was harder.

Say it's akin to utterance, not speech, not anything grammatical, not planned but simply received as thanks or love or gifts are received, involuntary as a scream or groaning or the gasps and moans of lovers in the act, daring the madman you've become to make a mockery of all restraint, vexing you the more to struggle to recall the unrecallable, random as fury and ending only when the storm is spent and even then not totally because it comes again in dreams when all evasion and deception and hypocrisy are inadmissible, and you remain its all too humble hostage where nothing but its power over you can free you to become the man you were before it chose you long enough to do what no one else could do.

He lay sprawled beside a parked Ford, its passenger door open. Beside him were broken eggs spilling from a torn shopping bag. I knelt and asked him, "Are you in pain any-where?" His lips said no. There was no voice. "I'll help you stand." His lips said yes, but still no voice. I gripped him under both armpits and lifted dead weight. Even for an old man, he weighed more than I thought. We tried again until he stood erect, but feebly. I steered him past the open door and slowly helped him seat himself. This time I heard his lips thank me. The woman behind the wheel frowned and muttered, "He broke the eggs, and then I called 911, and now they'll wonder why I called." When I said nothing, she told me to shut the door. Then she reversed and sped away. The man I had chosen to be in order to do what I'd chosen to do became the man who never would have done a thing. "If they find out he's hurt, you'll be to blame, and then they'll even make you pay for the eggs." He's always there with after-the-fact remarks like that, unlikely but possible.

She spoke of her son who biked from Pittsburgh to Guatemala to show it could be done. Three years later he pedaled the same three thousand miles to prove it could be done twice. I listened closely but said nothing. Record-setters leave me unenthused. Roger Bannister's sub-four-minute mile fades like an echo beside Mantle's longest homer (it counted only for a run) and all the necklaced gold of Spitz and Phelps. Once worn, the medals wear the wearers. I praise indifferent honorees... Awarded his prize in public, a winner of the Heisman Trophy (John Huarte of Notre Dame) hurried offstage to where his parents were seated. Only after kissing his mother and father did he return onstage to thank the judges, his coach and teammates. Had I a daughter, I'd want a man like that for her.

After Barbara told her friend Mary, "You'd like to think you love him, but you don't," nothing was the same between them. Barbara was right, but neither she nor Mary could foresee the result. At such moments it's not what's said but *how* it's said that matters. I have one friend who knows exactly when I've written unauthentic words or lines. She'll tell me frankly, "This doesn't sound like you." Later when I see how right she was, I willingly revise from scratch. This proves to me that making anyone aware of imperfections is an art that must inspire self-correction, not compliance or conformity. Leeway for genius has its place, but that depends on what's involved. With truth at stake, we need creative patience to make better what's never good enough.

I still am or used to be the following: son, grandson, son-in-law, godson, cousin, uncle, grandfather, godfather, citizen, sap, brother, brother-in-law, wastrel, officer, veteran, fool, student, teacher, sucker, scholar, dean, bargainer, tourist, dissenter, outsider, jackass, witness, senior, junior, patient, winner, loser, alumnus, finalist, next-of-kin, descendent, joker, relative, owner, editor, beneficiary, victim, protector, bluffer, distractor, debater, clown and nonagenarian in prospect who's nearing the exit where the title of "the late" awaits.

Thinking ahead, I see them suddenly older. Sam might be married to a quiet girl from Kansas or Tennessee or somewhere other than here. Anna might be singing on tour. Sarah as Sarah will be Sarah as ever and Sarah forever. I'll be a genuine dodderer by then, if I'm still doddering at all. Instead of feeling happy, I'll feel condemned to feel the old fears I felt once for their father. Will there be an accident?

Will some disease take them before they're twenty-one? Will they still love each other as they love each other now? This grandfather role is not what I expected. I cope with aging and concern no better than I cope with death and love. Nothing changes but the names.

The latter ages of man: after sixty, an obsession with being less gray, less balding, less old. After seventy, an awareness of malfunction, be it urinary, ocular or auditory coupled with the usual compensatory aids, i.e., eye glasses or lenses, hearing aids and so on. After eighty, a need for challenges, self-imposed or accidental, as a way to keep from becoming cynical or indifferent. After ninety, gratitude for loves and kindnesses known, unlimited gratitude, followed by a certainty, essentially mathematical, that every man's saga on this planet is finite and that the finite is chronologically nearer by the day.

Poems are rarely complete on arrival. Alternatives that could have been pursued insist they're still available. Saying "What's one is done" is true for history but not for poetry. History's beyond revision. Results, intended or not, prevail. These lines I'm writing now demand an ending, but the ending's not in sight. It leaves me wondering if poems that were never meant to end should be abandoned. Likewise, paintings. But unfinished paintings and unfinished symphonies survive as classics, regardless. The problem for poems is that they never really begin until they end. An ending gives a poem its entirety. No ending? No meaning. No poem.

Making love when you have no desire for it is like eating
when you're not hungry. It satisfies but never gratifies,
and gratitude is all that counts where love really matters.
Everything short of that is pleasure without meaning or
transcendence. The animal in us never sees the difference,
but the person—the human being—who we are does.

Properly and sacramentally understood the church is the
mystical body of Christ. Since we all are one with Christ,
and Christ is God, we are all of that body. As an organiza-
tion the church is composed of a hierarchy, man-created
and staffed by men. If I were an individual in that organi-
zation, I would bridle to be called "Your Eminence," "Your
Grace" or "Your Anything." Official vanity, all of it. It's like
what passes for the world where government resembles a
business, where universities resemble corporations, and
the church resembles a monarchy where all the grada-
tions and pieties associated with them prevail. Whoever
said that heaven was or is up? Christ said explicitly that
"the kingdom of heaven is within you," and Omar
Khayyam said that hell is there as well. And what of all this
banking of and on indulgences, plenary and otherwise?
Martin Luther posted his rejections on the door of a
church to claim that there were no calendars or promis-
sory notes in heaven. Why keep the risen Christ forever
nailed and sculpted on a cross? Why memorialize a hor-
rific execution every time we bless ourselves? If death had
come by hanging, would we be making the sign of the
noose?

"Tell everyone you chose to go to college so you could say
you'd gone. Or that you'd gone so you could say you went.
Either way it sounds impermanent. You'll pay for knowl-

edge on demand—not knowledge sought and found and then imagined into something totally original. You'll write by pushing buttons on a keyboard. Handwriting like discussion will be out of fashion. No one will note how handwritten letters are linked while those in print exist separately—a small point but not ignorable. You'll dawdle over multiple choice and choose the one least likely to be wrong. You'll look for answers but forget that questions are the only answers when the answers are beyond us. You'll call creative confusion a loss and not the beginning of wisdom. Tested but not educated, you'll be employable but bored, impatient, older and in debt."

My car has a mind of its own. It beeps if any other car is closer than it should be. A bulb will keep on blinking if a door's not locked. The clock on the dash can tell when Daylight Saving Time begins. It changes settings on schedule by itself. Like everyone, I use whatever innovates without a second thought. Specialists tell us, "Writing with just the index finger rather than with the whole hand 'no longer stimulates the neurons or the same cortical areas.'" If I still praise the power of pen and ink, some never-to-be-penmen say, "Who needs it?" Tired of stairways? Escalate in silence. Distressed by premature wrinkles? Leave them to surgeons. Coping with foes? Think nuclear. The more we improvise, the less we feel relieved. For better or worse, our preference for ease determines whether we change and when.

Driving left-sided from London to Stratford-on-Avon, I turned more British by the mile. After we saw *The Taming of the Shrew*, my son said, "He tamed the shrew, but he turned into the shrew." Later I viewed Shakespeare's signature (value: $5,000,000) in a letter—a pitch for money from a lord... After fifty summers, I'm remembering. It's past midnight. Yesterday's not over, and what's becoming today demands the verdict of the sun to be official. I'm wondering how many millions through five centuries saw or could have seen *The Taming of the Shrew*. Or why a dead man's name inscribed five hundred years ago should keep the man himself ongoing as a play—as if the ink's not dry.

The walls seem nearer. Barefooted on a Persian carpet, I walk on Asia Minor down the hall to the kitchen. The stove clock is telling time for no one. It's totally night, and a siren somewhere says the world's the same. Otherwise, stillness. My palm befriends a chair as further proof that I'm a man in the dark who has to feel his way through space alone. If what I feel's more dream than fact, so be it. I've had my fill of birthdays, anniversaries and other myths. Time, the murderer, decrees that those who live by the clock shall die by the clock. Here in my chosen darkness, I find a truer world where everything's much more itself when it's just near enough to touch.

Each trumpeter is over sixty-five. The average age of all the rest—except the drummer—is fifty-five. Their artistry is far from perfect but not exactly unexpected since retired secretaries, dentists, salesmen and nurses make up this township's band. Sousa's "Semper Fidelis" show them at their best. Judged by performance alone, the ages of the players mean nothing. Wherever the music takes them makes them put their differences aside while fervently attempting to be perfect for the music's sake.

One half of him survives. The other half's with her and will be always. The life she wakened in him with a smile or touch is gone. Since death exempts the heart, he finds his love for her enduring as an intimate but different nearness. When life becomes no more than living on, the presence of her absence saves him. By losing one he chose as he himself was chosen, he sleeps at the mercy of merciless dreams. Each dawn he asks how soon, how long?

Like silence in motion, she walked the way a woman with a purpose walks. He thought of that the night he asked her to dance. "Thanks, but make them change the music." He felt what poets say they when a poem they're trying to write refuses to be written. The music changed. Whatever it became inspired her to tap her toe to the rhythm. She turned her head to him the way a woman with a purpose turns to let the poem she is hiding happen. "Dance with me now," she said.

He had the window seat. After take-off he said, "My line is socks; what's yours?" I said I was a writer. He smiled his least impressive smile and asked, "What do you write?" I paused and said, "I hope they are poems." "Where are you headed now?" he added. I told him I'd been invited to recite my poems at a university. "They pay you for that?"

It was ten degrees above zero and snowing. Both of us were heading for class—I in my overcoat, he in shirtsleeves. "You need a coat," I said. "I don't participate in winter," he responded. "Even when it's near zero?" I persisted. "I never participate in winter."

John Berger: "If a talented artist cannot see or think beyond the decadence of the culture to which he belongs, if the situation is as extreme as ours, his talent will only reveal negatively but unusually vividly the nature and extent of that decadence. His talent will reveal, in other words, how it itself has been wasted."

Aside from *A Moveable Feast* and *The Old Man and the Sea*, I had to will myself to read Hemingway's later novels. The style was just as terse, but style and subject rarely matched. Books sold, regardless. Tidbits of fact made news because his name alone (plus beard) was news: Paris and the D'Angleterre, the plane crash he survived, the story of Ava Gardner swimming naked in his Finca Vigia pool, the Nobel Prize, the gunshot in Idaho. Since what makes news makes money, the hucksters hyped as tribute what they labeled with his name: hunting jackets, rum, a Mont Blanc pen, champagne, beard oil, chairs, coffee and a Fuente cigar...

I no longer have the will to cope with Thomas Aquinas, Emerson, Plato or Camus. Not that they're wanting.... They have no equals. But total concentration has its limits, and most philosophies perplex as much as they console me. Aesop saw problems as fables, while all eight of Shakespeare's fools plus Shakespeare himself made poems of the lot. Facing the same dilemmas, Mark Twain became a humorist. Perhaps this shows that words spoken (or words unsaid but felt) outlive words printed and read. Or why the pain of tragedy transformed into fables or plays, survives as wisdom or poetry. Or how Mark Twain saw something comic at the worst of times and laughed and smoked his pipe and laughed again.

Lapsing into lies, the lips succumb, but the eyes—never. Why else is looking someone in the eye the ultimate proof of honesty? Or seeing eye to eye a synonym for trust? The ears must wait for words or sounds to come to them, but eyes can roam, and the sky's the limit. I leave to oculists the lexicon of pupils, retinas and irises. Seeing's more than sighting. The eyes disdain, invite or spurn without disguise. Love spoken by the eyes is love at its deepest. For lovers the eyes can seem to touch, embrace and kiss. But eyes are coy. Wounds inflicted by the eyes refuse to heal. Eyes understand and speak in silence. Cornered by hatred, the eyes can stab at will. And they can kill.

Retiring, the weatherman sees that time for him was always time passing. His job was having to decide how much of what was possible was likely. He saw yesterdays as tomorrows that happened. Tomorrows were yesterdays to come. He took the blame for everything he overlooked: rain that spoiled an outdoor wedding, lightning that struck a steeple, overnight snow that clotted traffic for hours. But then foretelling anything was always three-parts luck…. No more of that for him. He's on his own. No one can blame him for anything. He's through with seeing time as history where nothing stands still. He has new things to do and think about. There's more to life than weather. If it rains so what? If not, so what?

We know them by name. They're more than mere acquaintances. We swap hellos. We send each other cards. We share discreet amazement over the spectacular vermilion of a wild cherry in October or the distance in light years from Pennsylvania to Mars. We never bare to them or share our hopes or hells…. When troubles happen to reveal how dear they are to us, and we to them, we put aside what once was mere politeness. We read each other's eyes. Instead of chatting, we confide.

It's sentry-time. Framed pictures keep the walls from being boring. The house is talking to itself in French. Outside a car passes as if reluctant to be a lone car moving after midnight. Everything seems irrelevant as yesterday's weather. This time is not the time the clocks are telling tock by tick. It's more like moments spent recovering from agony or loss, or writing by hand a letter that must be written, or letting the mind become as open as possible to prove that nothing's better than to be—-simply to be.

I turned cross-traffic. A trooper waved me to a stop. The closer he came the more he became the Marine sergeant I knew in Portsmouth.

"Fowler," I said.

"Well, loo-tenant, what if it ain't."

"No alibi, my fault."

"Cutting cross-traffic like that rates a hundred-dollar ticket."

"No excuses."

"What do you think I ought to do, loo-tenant?"

"It's up to you, Fowler."

He smiled the smile of authority and added slowly, "I didn't like you then, and I don't like you now, but just for old time's sake I think I'll let you go."

They look pensive as out-patients waiting to be diagnosed or cleared for release. For them the future is where the fates they fear the most are waiting to happen. Explaining that what's possible need not be seen as imminent or likely since death can come as instantly at twenty as at ninety eases nothing. Every birthday arrows the odds until they're totally aged by age... I find myself recalling how my son and his godmother could be together and silent for hours but totally happy. Separated by sixty years, they wanted nothing more than being near each other. I'd ever seen a purer love. Their time together was time enough for anyone to see that time, when counted or feared but never shared, is time lost.

False prophets in the *Farmer's Almanac* can keep their fortune-telling to themselves. After four days of June weather in February the daffodils are up and blooming. Some say that winter flowers seldom last because the frost that's bound to come will come. I've heard the same words said of people who defiantly endure to make the unbelievable believable. This proves that doing what's never been done seems normal only after someone does it.... Totally in bloom, the daffodils are now too busy being daffodils to know the difference.

Dawn: "It's wiser to ignore knowingly than to confront an enemy. Confrontations can result in something totally different than what you expected."

What shocks you to a stop like someone shot denies denial. You're left wounded and alone. You long to be the man you were, but he's no longer you. You lose all interest in travel, comfort and money. You watch the televised world worsen by the day—a President exceedingly exceeds excess—a massive tornado levels central Oklahoma

—a mother's severed arm cradles a dead baby in Aleppo. Some say the world could be redeemed by mass allegiance to religion. Because religion stands for ritual, tradition and obedience, that seems as far from faith as reason is from revelation. It's not at peace with irony, which, according to Aristotle, is the essence of life as it is lived. This leaves you doing what you're doing now—handwriting in a notebook with a fountain pen so you *feel* what you're thinking and seeing.

When our son brought him home, he could fit in a coffee cup—a peekapoo puppy he named Oscar. Actually, he chose the dog for his mother; he simply thought that they would make a good pair. As Oscar grew, he and Mary Anne would "sing" duets. He would sit on her lap and croon Pagliacci's lament. He was the baritone; she, the soprano. Even when the duet was supposed to end, he would keep crooning until he tired to a whimper. When Viveca Genaux, who sang at the Met, asked Oscar to sing with her, he yawned. Like all dogs, Oscar was allergic to hypocrisy. If bored, he let it show. If not, he turned defiant. If someone came between him and Mary Anne, it was war at first sight. Hours before he died, he searched the house for her as if he wanted no one else but her to hear his final song.

You answer to your name but rarely with a smile. Your mirror proves you're not who you were. When cashing checks or crossing borders, you let your ID's and driver's license speak on your behalf. The problem is that you're the problem. Rather than feeling more yourself each year, you feel the opposite. You focus on shopping or paying bills for distraction. They both rank low on the scale of values, but low is better than nothing when all the chips are down. You've long since known that life concludes for everyone as scripted. Not knowing *when* is bad enough. Not knowing *how* is worse.

Flashing flag-pins from lapels, the rivals order God to "bless America." They ought to know (but don't) that language loses in fervor what it gains in bombast. It's like comparing love vowed in a whisper with love proclaimed in High C above High C. Or "I love you" handwritten with "I LOVE YOU" skywritten in space by a pilot in a Piper Cub. Fervor is not inclined to bow to anyone called Your Eminence, Your Highness or Your So-and-So, or honor honors never earned, or trust those who say "Trust me," or take as true all smiles smiled for photographers....

A granddaughter writes about bathing her grandmother in bed. The grandmother says she know it's a bother. The granddaughter say she loves doing it and kisses her. They embrace, and the tears come. There's something more than kinship here—more than need, kindness or appreciation. It proves the heart is more than just a muscle. It's what speaks finally in eloquent silence. It happens when the body slackens or sickens slowly to the last surrender. And the heart resists.

Richard ("If the President does it, it's not illegal") Nixon was pardoned by Gerald Ford to spare the country the "agony of a trial." Let's put aside for the sake of argument that more than half of the 58,000 Americans killed in Vietnam died after Nixon took office in 1968 on the pledge to end the war. Put aside his "incursion" into Cambodia ("Bomb the bastards") as well as Nelson Rockefeller's in-

sight into Nixon's "peevishness" and historian Richard
Hofstadter's linking Nixon to what Hofstadter called the
"paranoid style in American politics." That leaves Watergate. Watergate alone as exposed by Robert Woodward
and Carl Bernstein and adjudicated by Judge John Sirica
was a direct assault on constitutional government, which
is as close to "high crimes and misdemeanors" as even the
most devoted of Nixon's admirers would have to concede.
But in light of Ford's pardon, justice was never served.
Nixon's underlings were sentenced for what Nixon orches-
trated....while Nixon remained *beyond* the law.

Testifying before the Senate under oath in the uniform of a
Marine officer, Lt. Colonel Oliver North lied about the Iran-
Contra deal, in which money from Iran was diverted to the
Contras on Nicaragua. The entire scheme bypassed the
Boland Amendment as well as Congressional approval and
oversight and created a precedent that led Reagan, who
claimed to know nothing of the matter, to fire North. After
his trial, an Appeals Court reversed North's three convic-
tions and commuted his three-year sentence. Suddenly
finding himself *beyond* the law, North ran for a Senate seat
from Virginia, lost a close election to Chuck Robb and
moved on to hosting television programs on Fox news devoted to military heroes and giving speeches for fat fees to
evangelical audiences. The higher-ups who approved of
North's actions—Admiral John Poindexter, Eliot Abrams
and Caspar Weinberger—were duly pardoned by President George H. W. Bush. Placed *beyond* the law, Abrams
went on to influence Middle East policies in the administration of Bush *fils*, despite the fact that Abrams' biases in
the area were widely known. It seems that when a man

like Abrams is *beyond* the law, he is also beyond disqualification.

NO ONE TO BLAME BUT THE BLAMERS

No one believed it would happen.
No one denied it was so.
The months were the same,
and the mail still came,
and a green light still meant go.

If anyone raised an objection,
the leader said little or less.
The standard deceivers
deceived the believers,
and nobody trusted the press.

So, life went along as it used to,
and the sun still set in the west.
The stock profits grew.
nd the flags still flew,
and everyone hoped for the best

The end when it came made us wonder
what happened to cause all the fuss.
The more that we neared
the fear that we feared,
the more it appeared to be us.

The red Pontiac had been tailing me before I reached the Holland Tunnel. The driver looked both furious and exasperated. Twice he tried to pass, but traffic made it impossible. He was alone, and I could see in the rear-view mirror that he was talking, probably swearing. All the way through the tunnel he stayed as close as a yard behind me, occasionally blaring his horn for the hell of it. Once out of the tunnel, he pulled alongside, rolled down his window and said, "You never let me pass, and now we're tied. What good did it do you?"

"Nora, I love to travel, but George hates it." "So?" "He's never going to change." "Why not just accept it?" "I try, but it's not easy." "Listen, honey, Fred was five inches shorter than I was when we got married, and he still is." "And?" "In bed it makes no difference."

Unlike women named for flowers (Rose, Lily or Dahlia) or virtues (Hope, Prudence or Faith) or saints (Joan, Frances or Mary), my three good friends are Sloan, Shea and Paige. With just one syllable their names can charm. Men's names like Max, Gus or Sam fall flat, but Sloan, Shea and Paige are up and running. Max says, "Let's go."Sloan says, "Let's not." Gus says, "Let's work." Shea says, "Let's dance." Sam says, "Let's choose." Paige says, "Let's talk." Lately a fourth outcharms all three when she purrs who I am with her look-at-me look. She's Paige's baby sister. Name's Brooke...

Catherine de Medici was responsible for the creation of the perfume industry in France after she told the leather workers in the South of France that they should create a less malodorous product than uncured leather. The leatherworkers tried to compromise by perfuming the leather. That was shortlived. Finally, having access to jasmine that was bountiful in the area (jasmine was then and still is the essence of perfumes of all scents), they focused on perfume as their favored industry. France's largest and most profitable export remains perfume. Catherine de Medici also liked the taste of a sherbet that was made in Genoa, and she brought that to France as well.

Susan Sontag: "The painter constructs; the photographer discloses."

Pablo Picasso: "Everything you can imagine is real."

The vaudevillian catfights that masquerade as presidential elections every four years have often prompted many to ask, "How did we get to this point?" Perhaps the best way to address (if not answer) this question is to consider what our country has become in the last fifty or so years. First, the effects of war. Since the end of World War II but particularly since 1965, we have become inured to the daily death counts and casualty lists created by war. The approximate total number of American war-deaths from 1965 to the present is more than 66,000. The wounded along with civilian deaths reach a much higher number. Meanwhile those in the population of Vietnam, Afghanistan and Iraq that we have killed is over two million. This has prompted some historians to claim that we have killed more people in the last fifty or so years than any other nation. The irony is that these presidentially chosen wars have now been shown to have had no legal or moral justification. Nothing reveals this more succinctly than George W. Bush's answer to Richard B. Clark, Chairman of the Counterterrorism Group, when Clark questioned the legality of the invasion of Iraq that Bush was determined to launch. "I don't care what the international lawyers say," Bush bragged, "we are going to kick some a—." So began the ongoing deterioration of the Middle East on orders from a former collegiate cheerleader. That seems blameworthy enough but even more blameworthy are those who never charged Bush judicially with taking the country to war unjustifiably. Lyndon Johnson benefitted from the same legal disregard over his hyping the war in Vietnam for cooked-up reasons. One result of this is that we have become a people inured to indifference to the law by elected officials while simply accepting the reverberating effects that such indifference has on other aspects of our very lives.

I often wonder if our resignation to military deaths is related to our acceptance of homicides at home–approximately 80 per day. I wonder also if the military's reliance on force as a problem-solver is related to the self-arming of the population. At this writing the number of guns in the country outnumbers the census—300,000,000 plus. The effect of war on the outlook of citizens has been accompanied by a change in demographics since what Arthur Miller called the "Reagan trance." In the 1980's the wealthy constituted about 10% of the population. By the end of the Reagan administration that figure was close to doubling while the Lower Middle Class (the poor) increased from 20% to 30%. In terms of arithmetic this means that the Middle Class had shrunk...and the Middle Class is America at work. What were the results? One of the results was that young men unable to find work were joining the military as a viable option with its promise of the G. I. Bill and sizable bonuses for extension. This in turn enriched the pool of servicemen to be committed to another presidentially chosen war. The Pentagon, which has a larger public relations budget than any comparable government or fiscal institution on the face of the earth, cooperated with incentive advertising and other inducements to enlistment and extension. The reality is that an all-volunteer military assures compliance without dissent. The dark side to this is that repeated deployments in dangerous areas might have a connection to the number of suicides of men on active duty (some 300 per year). Among veterans (including Iraq and Afghanistan veterans) the rate is more than 20 per day.

For young people not involved in the military, the most desirable option is a college education. With room, board and tuition running annually from $30,000 to more than $65,000 plus clothing and travel, only the wealthy or those resigned to a lifetime of debt can cope with collegiate costs. Noam Chomsky even implies that some universities may be heightening costs and becoming more concerned with profit than education. I would like not to believe this, but there is no question that the lenders are profiting and that the student-debtors become more concerned with debt remission than with dissent on public issues. Whether they are complicit or not, the universities may be curbing public dissent on war policies by graduating students whose first concern is debt reduction. It's worth thinking about. The final contributor to public distrust in government is our tolerance of pressures from foreign governments and domestic lobbyists over American foreign policy. Client nations like Saudi Arabia and Israel are constantly striving to have our interests made identical with their own. The Saudis, where no one without a spermatic link with the governing "royal family" has a real voice, remain displeased over American détente with Iran and our pleas for restraint in Yemen. The Israelis went so far as to collude with Republican political leaders to have Prime Minister Netanyahu speak to a joint session of Congress in opposition to the Iran issue and other matters. Obama, who had not even been told of the invitation, said nothing to denounce this open insult to the Presidency itself, prompting the distinguished Afro-American scholar and author Cornel West to call Obama "Nelson Rockefeller in blackface." Sixty members of Congress proved themselves defiantly offended (as expressed by Congressman Earl Blumenauer of Oregon on You-Tube) by not attending the speech that was greeted by robot-like standings and sittings and applause by the obsequious attendees. Lately a Las Vegas billionaire named Adelson with a fortune fleeced from suckers at Casino games has pledged $100,000,000 to Trump to influence Middle East policy while his counterpart, a Hollywood producer named Saban, has pledged comparable millions to Hillary Clinton for the same purpose. All such "contributions" are legally sacrosanct now because of the Supreme Court's 5-4 passage of Citizens United, which equates political gifting with free speech so that "money" now literally "talks." Facing the options, voters are increasingly being urged to choose the lesser evil. This is nothing but a craven escape masquerading as a conscientious alternative. Evil is presented as just another abstract noun. But just suppose the options had to do with relief from constipation, and the sufferer was offered two equally repugnant laxatives and asked to choose. Political constipation is our present condition, and the present "laxatives" being offered do not promise much more than a prolongation, not a cure. None of the aforementioned pressures on our national life shows signs of vanishing. Neo-con greed is firmly ensconced. The historian Tony Judt has stated accurately, "We have pursued our self-interest (defined as maximum economic advantage) with minimal reference to extraneous criteria such as altruism, self-denial, taste, cultural habit or collective purpose." The policies of the New Deal and the progressive legislation of the early 1960's were altruistic at the core, and the country as a whole benefitted from Social Security, the G. I. Bill of Rights, Medicare, Medicaid, the Civil Rights Bill, Headstart, Student Loans, the Peace Corps, Food Stamps, the National Endowment for the Arts, the National Endowment for the Humanities and the Corporation for Public Broadcasting. There's been nothing as altruistic since.

It was Anatole France who said, "To know is nothing; to imagine is everything." Some have interpreted this statement to mean that knowledge and imagination are opposed. I rather see it as two different but not contradictory ways of acknowledging and identifying the world. One is static; the other is kinetic. One perceives; the other envisions. One names; the other, re-names. What results are two different ways of experiencing reality. One recognizes appearances; the other, essences. For example, it is one thing to say that all genuine loves can never be forgotten. It is another to say, as John Donne said, "I cannot say I loved, for who can say /He was killed yesterday." The statement about love in the first instance is clear but hardly evocative. It is plain prose. It can easily be forgotten. The lines by John Donne evoke rather than define. They also incline to be memorable because they induce the reader to complete the metaphor. They suggest that the lover, like someone who has been killed, cannot assume that his death has not happened. Similarly, the philosopher-poet Kahlil Gibran indirectly considered envy in an imaginative way by describing the effect of envy on behavior: "The silence of the envious is too noisy." Those who are literally minded may or may not see or react to such indirection, but imaginatively they are the losers. H. L. Mencken went so far as to link envy with puritanism. Puritanism has been defined as scrupulous control or even denial of the human appetites, particularly those related to sex. Mencken tried to see beyond the *what* into the *why* of puritanism. Was it merely asceticism or something more? He finally concluded that a puritan may be haunted or prompted in denial by "the fear that someone, somewhere, may be happy."

These few examples reveal a basic truth that we ignore at our peril. William Blake revealed it when he wrote: "We are led to believe a lie/When we see not through but with the eye." Seeing *with* the eye is seeing, shall we say, photographically. Seeing *through* the eye means seeing imaginatively, seeing more than appearances, seeing the face behind the mask. Perhaps the best way to distinguish the difference between the two ways of seeing (*with* or *through* the eye) is to focus on the difference between journalism (news reporting) and literature. News reporting focuses on the facts, i.e., who, what, where and when. Literature is the author's imaginative expression of the facts in a way that goes beyond who, what, where and when. Here is but one example of two different ways of acknowledging the same reality. Lester Maddox was the Governor of Georgia in the late 1960's. A strong segregationist, he distributed axe handles to his white constituents so they could use them or threaten to use them on black citizens when they attempted to vote or eat in public restaurants. Such are the facts. And Maddox himself in all his righteousness would often be photographed in solidarity with his axe-holding constituents, scowling and otherwise displaying his defiance. Norman Mailer described the truculent attitude of the man (as well as of all his followers) with a single sentence: "Lester Maddox has the face of a mean baby with glasses on it."

Maddox and all his followers lacked the imaginative vision to understand that the United States at its foundation broke with lineage, race, ethnicity or other forms of tribalism as the basis of nationality. The Declaration of Independence, which originated in Thomas Jefferson's imagination, left no doubt of what it meant to be an American citizen: "We hold these truths to be self-evident, that all men are created equal, that they are endowed by their Creator with certain inalienable rights, that among these are Life, Liberty and the pursuit of happiness." Regardless, the belief in white supremacy has always been an under-current in American public life.

Mere debate about racial equality will probably be ongoing and end with the same tensions. On the other hand, a more imaginative consideration might lead to a less confrontational conclusion. But the imagination must have a place in this social question, particularly regarding the essence of what the "self-evident" truths are and what those who are opposed to that think they are. As a parallel consider the condition of Ireland in 1919. The country was fracturing, and it took a poem by William Butler Yeats to show what was at stake. In his poem called "The Second

Coming" these few lines present what was undeniable: "Things fall apart; the centre cannot hold;/ Mere anarchy is loosed upon the world,/The blood-dimmed tide is loosed, and everywhere/The ceremony of innocence is drowned,/The best lack all conviction, while the worst/ Are full of passionate intensity." The picture of disintegration in these lines could apply to any society that is coming (or could come) apart. And a select number of American and foreign poets have been writing poems, as Yeats wrote in his era, where imagination becomes visionary, politically and otherwise. Philip Booth, for example, wrote how a realtor's attempt to gentrify a neighborhood prompted him to create "desert dusty streets with fertile names." Robert Lowell, contemplating downtown traffic in Boston, saw a "savage servility slide by on grease." A similar clairvoyance prompted Derek Walcott from his home in St. Lucia to declare for his fellow Caribbeans, "We are a nation, or we are nothing." And there is Linda Pastan's poetic refutation of those who say we should live each day as if it were our last day. Preferring to see each day (correctly) as our first, she writes: "I set/the table, glance out the window/where dew has baptized every/living surface." And finally there is W. S. Merwin's incomparable farewell to a lost thought: "Coming late, as always,/I try to remember what I almost heard./The light avoids my eye./How many times have I head the locks close/And the lark take the keys/And hang them in heaven." These few examples show how language born of the imagination does surface in our day-to-day speech along with the language of mere talk or factual communication, though certainly not as often. Imagination in advertising is, of course, bountiful, but it is imagination for commercial purposes. Its aim is to seduce for the purpose of inciting the seduced to purchase a product. Some of it is memorable, to be sure, but it is not memorable in the best sense—as something remembered because it touches something in the soul. It is one thing to say that "Pepsi Cola hits the spot." It is something else to say, as Robert Frost said, "Ah, when to the heart of man/Was it less than a treason/To go with the drift of things,/To yield with a grace to reason/And bow and accept the end/Of a love or a season?" Or Frost's equally memorable but often misinterpreted—"I took the road less travelled by/and that has made all the difference."

A close friend of mine now in his mid-nineties wrote me a letter recently in which this line appeared "Knowing is stifling; not knowing is creative." Up to that point in the letter he had been commenting on how men deal with the inescapable fact of their inevitable deaths. Knowing in advance that they will die, they varied in their reactions. Some, knowing that death could come at any time, Opted to live stoically, fearfully but unwaveringly and even penitentially with this knowledge . Others, accepting the same logic, reacted by creating a life of their choice in what they saw as the time given or remaining. In the first instance, knowledge of death's certainty resulted in a kind of paralysis. In the second, not knowing when death would occur freed men to pursue alternatives that could be both creative and fulfilling. I found myself totally in agreement with my friend's statement about the stifling effect of knowing compared to the creative release of not knowing, but I could not understand why. How could knowledge be considered stifling when so many sources and institutions in our society exist to provide it? Without succumbing to the Faustian bargain of wanting to know everything (being totally knowledgeable), I knew and know from my own experience that generally we prefer to know than not know. After all, we live in a world obsessed with a belief in the ultimate value of information and a preference for the factual over the obscure or the mysterious. But I saw how factual knowledge could have a stifling effect. For instance, it is scientifically correct that the speed of an object in free-fall is thirty-two feet per second per second. But where do we go after that? And even the most assiduous pursuer of knowledge must concede that the odds against omniscience are not in his favor. "What you know is what you do not know," wrote T. S. Eliot, "and that is all you know."

Since ours is a culture where the language of communication (everything from conversation to journalism to expository prose) far outweighs the language of communion (poetic statements and literature generally), it's not time wasted if we consider their differences. The language of communication inundates us daily via television, radio and in newsprint as well as in the various ways we use words in conversation. But this language engages us cognitively, and on balance we hear and then forget most of it. For as long as it lasts, this language can be stifling in the sense that it crowds out everything else. But rarely does it affect us feelingly. It's here and gone.

Months ago, I watched a television program composed of interviews with wives and mothers of soldiers killed in combat. One of those interviewed was the mother of a captain killed by a sniper. She recounted how she received a letter from him postmarked on the day he was killed. She said that she read it often since it contained his last words. Each time she put the letter back in the envelope, she slowly licked it shut so that she could taste her son in the last thing he touched. Those were her exact words. Obviously, she never knew in advance how she would react, but hearing her say what she actually did made her story spiritually and emotionally accessible to anyone who heard it.

If not knowing is creative, the reason is that it is as spontaneous as it is surprising and irrepressible. The imagination is suddenly actuated. Poems are the most obvious examples of what results from this kind of feeling/thinking. They are created by inspiration at the moment of the poet's not knowing what to say or write until the inspired words come to him gratis. He creates the poem word by word as it grows within him according to its own laws so that in a sense he is transformed into just an instrument for its creation. It's in the not knowing what he feels impelled to say that the energy of creation exists.

Such imaginative epiphanies are not reserved only for poets. Every human being is capable of experiencing a poetic moment and of trying to create (or re-create) a previously unknown experience that is his imaginative answer to something not previously known. Many years ago my then eight-year-old son was bouncing a ball in the driveway. While he was doing it, he turned to me and said, "Look, Dad, I'm making the ball happy." In another instance my nine-year-old niece said the following to her father while he was playfully holding her by the ankles, "Daddy, please let go of my wrist-legs." Not knowing the correct noun, she created her own phrase, and it strikes me frankly as better. I could go on and cite other instances where not knowing had equally creative benefits as opposed to merely knowing or following a tradition. But it was the rebellious imagination that was responsible for the changes in each instance. This imaginative rebellion goads us into action when we are simply inclined to accept what we have gotten used to. In this sense it can be said that we more or less deserve what we choose to get used to—preferring the already known instead of responding to the challenge of the unknown. What it finally comes down to is that life is by nature not static. It is ultimately a mystery that has more in common with what we do not or cannot know than what we do know. Dogmatic and catechetical answers are not helpful here. One theologian once told me that looking for certainty in matters of faith or hope comes from a psychological and not a truly spiritual need. That points to the sterility of all fundamentalisms. And this is why the creative imagination for those who accept the human condition of not knowing is the only reliable agent to create change. Those who have the imaginations to create new realities where the outcomes are both unknown and unforeseeable are the true visionaries whether they be poets, children, statesmen, scientists or educators.

THE HOMELAND DEFENDERS

"We're fighting them there so that we don't have to fight them here."

——A Homelander's Motto

"An American soldier dies every day and a half, on average, in Iraq or Afghanistan. Veterans kill themselves at a rate of one every 80 minutes. More than 6,500 veteran suicides are logged every year—more than the total number of soldiers killed in Afghanistan and Iraq combined since the war began."

——Nicholas Kristof

They tortured or killed the disrupters
of makeover plans they had made.
They pledged they had come to bring freedom.
They promised to leave, but they stayed.

They censored reports on the wounded.
They zippered the dead into bags.
They flew back the bodies like cargo
and sheeted their caskets with flags.

Of those who had backed the invasion,
ot one ever served in a war.
Evasion was more to their liking,
and that's what they opted for.

For them all that mattered was power,
and power meant bullets and guns.
But those whom they ordered to use them
were somebody else's sons.

With book deals and medals and pardons
they never looked back but ahead.
They swore to a man it was worth it,
and nobody mentioned the dead.

Truth always matters, but there are times when it matters
but more so. I think like this while a pair of pigeons watch
me as I stoke their feeder. Like non-violent "insisters" they
perch in place and wait to be acknowledged as pigeons,
not annoyances. They help me realize that less can mean
much to the least while much can matter least to the most.
They practice social distancing. After I leave, they feed until they've had their fill, then flex and taxi for a slow flight
beyond leftover seeds and houses and neighborhoods
where people are dealing with life and death and everything in between.

Here in western Pennsylvania we're a month past lock-
down as well as zones red and yellow, but the virus has
spiked again. The wearing of masks is re-required as well
as six feet of space between people in public places if and
when they leave their homes for necessities. When the re-
strictions first became part of daily life, I wanted to be
miraculously exonerated so that I could live what was, after all, my life. Gradually I came to realize that this was a
real emergency. The only time I could remember as being
similar was the era before Dr. Jonas Salk discovered the
polio vaccine. Masks and distancing were not relevant
then, and polio was always possible. If you didn't get it,
you were simply lucky. But the corona pandemic is different, and wanting to live as if you are singularly immune is
both naïve and dangerous to yourself and others. Eventually the question becomes what can you do and how do
you live in the meanwhile. There are basically two ways to
react to what is unignorable. (And I leave aside health
providers and all others who have to work to earn their
livings and provide for such necessities as food, medica-

tions, transportation and other needs for the general public). The first reaction is to become a stoic and "tough it
out." Stoics try to live as well as they can in semi-incarcer-
ation. Sooner rather than later they accept the merciless
fact that being human means that they are subject to what
is beyond their control. Distractions are possible, of
course, but the longing for the life they lived only intensifies over time. The one thing that sustains them is hope
and determination, interrupted now and then by pent up
impatience and some choice occasional cursing. The only
thing that can break this cycle is the power of the imagination since it is only the imagination that permits us to
transcend the circumstances in which we sometimes find
ourselves. This is not escapism. It is what permits us to
feel or see or hear what defies time and space with a reality that puts us in touch (or back in touch) with our humanity as if for the first time. It may be remembering an
incident or an unexpected kindness where you were the
beneficiary. It may be recalling an insight or a statement
that suddenly connected you with a truth that made everything else secondary. Such an insight came to me this
morning. I suddenly remembered an accident that happened when I was six years old. I was in Watertown, New
York, with my father. He was on a business trip to the
Thousand Islands, and he taken my brother and me with
him. We were walking together on a dock, and I began
running. I had only taken a few steps when I tripped and
fell into twenty feet of water. I had not yet learned how to
swim, and my father was not able to swim. All I remember
now was sinking slowly in lake water until I felt myself being lifted to the surface. It so happened that there was a
man on the dock who saw me trip, and he jumped fully
clothed into the water and saved me. Had it not been for

him—a total stranger—I would not be writing this. Even as I write, I think of the years between that moment and right now. In fact, I thought of that just before I decided to feed the pigeons as described at the beginning of this essay. The memory made the feeding more than a chore. I don't want to get sentimental about this, but it made what was ordinary more than ordinary. The fact that I was living through a pandemic came into a different and humane perspective. Over the years I've also thought often (and gratefully) about another incident that was serendipitous and life-changing. Thinking about it now during the pandemic is like going from ordinary prose to poetry. Spiritually I felt that kind of change.

Re-reading several books about Lincoln's address at Gettysburg, I learned something about the battle of Gettysburg that I not only did not know but never thought about, namely, that 5,000 horses were killed there.

The distinguished journalist Irvin S. Cobb was showing a guest his library. The guest was in awe of Cobb's collection and finally asked him, "Have you read every one of these?" Cobb answered ambiguously, "Some of them twice."

The Spaniards first brought Arabian stallions and mares to Mexico for military purposes. Year after year the Arabian horses began to interbreed with wild horses, and the interbred horses in turn grazed farther and farther north into what in time would become Texas, New Mexico, Oklahoma and all the other western states. These were the original mustangs and Appaloosas. The westering pioneers caught and trained these feral horses to their purposes, i.e., saddling them in their battles with Indian tribes, using them to pull covered wagons or ploughs, riding them to oversee herds of cattle and so on. Mustangs literally created our image of the cowboy.

Indians also found in the mustang a war horse. Mounted on mustangs, Sioux and Cheyenne tribes massacred Custer and his troops in the battle of the Little Big Horn in Montana in 1876. In one sense imagining the original "wild west" without the horse is like imagining the conquest of much of Europe by Genghis Khan without his reliance on the oriental mustang. The mustang became the very basis of military and agricultural power as well as the means of traveling from place to place. That reliance is commemorated to this day by the military's perpetuating the term "cavalry" and applying it to battalions of tanks that have long since replaced mustangs once used for such purposes. And "horsepower" is a term still in constant use to calculate the capacity of engines or motors that do what horses used to do. The mustang is central to all this. Most people think of the thoroughbred as the apogee of horses (in terms of purity of lineage he may well be). They were known for their speed. And they are beautiful to look at whether at rest or in full gallop. But in modern terms their speed becomes ignorable after they grow too old to compete in the Kentucky Derby or the Belmont. After that they are left to breed and graze. They are seen as the trophies of the wealthy. In a narrow aesthetic sense, a Seabiscuit or a Man of War makes a mustang or an Appaloosa look almost pedestrian. Mustangs seem like the bastard sons of kings who fought for and kept order in the kingdom while the legitimate but spoiled sons or thoroughbreds remained at court to serve the aristocracy. There is a hidden but unignorable metaphor in all this when applied to human societies and, particularly, to democracies. The mustang principle seems to prevail in respective forms of government. The illusion of purity of lineage is reduced to an ever lessening percentage as disparate groups associate, integrate and propagate. The result is not only the creation of a different population but one where ethnic assets of one group fructify in even more striking ways when integrated or fused with the assets of another. Those who resist or deny the existence of such a change in populations so affected would seem to be facing an unrealistic future. I am reminded of the royal families of yesteryear in Spain, for example, who, in order to keep the royal line "pure," would encourage and demand that cousins marry cousins and so forth. Hygienists could have warned them that such "human engineering" would weaken rather than strengthen such unions, resulting in everything from hemophilia to tremors.

Applying the mustang principle to the United States, it seems inevitable that the population will become as disparate as the intermingling of the ethnicities and races determines it will be. It will be, in brief, a nation of mustangs. Predictable resistance and displeasure to this will come from white supremacists, lineage purists and outright or introverted racists. This resistance will always be with us even though there is nothing in the Constitution that discriminates against races or ethnicities or even implies that anything but allegiance to the Constitution is the basis for American citizenship. While I was doing some background reading for this essay, I came across reference after reference to the ethnic background of Abraham Lincoln. However interesting this has been and will continue to be to some historians and sociologists, it simply has no place in our estimate of Lincoln as an American President who affirmed the equality of all men as well as a government of, by and for the people. That—and not ethnicity or race—is the basis of the United States of America. It is what has drawn disparate people here from all parts of the world. Once here they mingled and merged with one another to create a different population. The history of the mustang can offer some insight into that.

Most people would concede that what is truly important is what we cannot forget even if we try. These could be events, persons, places or words spoken or written. Unlike words, most events, persons and places tend to live on like aging photographs. We see them within the parentheses of years, months or days. Often to our regret they have dated lives. But memorable words seem to have an undying legacy, and they manage to survive the times and places of their origin without difficulty. How? Perhaps it is because they retain their original energy and express something that is permanently true. It is inherent in how Sophocles has Haimon answer his father Creon in *Antigone* after being reprimanded by Creon for having the temerity to correct his elders: "But if I am young and right, what difference does it make if I am young?" Or it could be St. Paul's, "Yea, though I speak with the tongues of men and angels and have not charity, I am become as sounding brass or a tinkling cymbal." Why have these words kept their original life? What makes them unforgettable? The answer may be contained in a letter that Robert Frost wrote to the philosopher Sidney Hook. Frost stressed in the letter that there is an essential difference between a grammatically correct sentence and a living sentence. He did not define the difference, but he suggested that a living sentence could be identified by its undismissable effect. I would suggest that one line from Robert Frost's "The Death of the Hired Man" would qualify as a living sentence: "Home is the place where, when you have to go there,/They have to take you in." And the same sense of life is present in the four sentences that constitute an early poem of Frost's entitled "November":

> We saw leaves go to glory,
> Then almost migratory
> Go part way down the lane,
> And then to end the story
> Get beaten down and pasted
> In a wild day of rain.
>
> We heard "'Tis over" roaring.
> A year of leaves was wasted.
> Oh, we make a boast of storing.
> Of saving and of keeping,
> But only by ignoring
> The waste of moments sleeping,
> The waste of pleasure weeping,
> By denying and ignoring
> The waste of nations warring.

These lines "live" because they succeed in expressing felt thought in all its fullness. They manage to let us share the feeling as we absorb the thought. We listen with our whole selves and not merely from the eyebrows up. All the words contribute to a unified poetic effect and persuade us that the expression is as perfect as possible for its purpose. It meets Henry David Thoreau's standard: "That which is done well once is done forever. It creates the power of the imperishable example. Its memorability follows from this. The words last as written or said because the inimitable has no substitutes. It lets itself be known by heart, which is the best form of knowledge because it confirms it as an ongoing presence.

The difference between the transitory and the permanent is obvious if we compare living or poetic lines with the following journalistic examples. "The idea of canning a huge, flavorful beer was anathema in the bottle-fetish craft-brewing world where cans were associated with mass-produced plonk." Or "Clint Eastwood takes an intimate look at the pubic face of war." Both of these sentences are grammatically correct, but all that they convey is information, as intended. Even a committee could have written them. The journalist I. F. Stone, who has been deservedly praised for indicting various politicians by using their own words against them, believed as a matter of political fact (and so wrote) that all politicians lie—some less skillfully than others, some adroitly, but all, shamelessly. Lying in its essence is not merely a trivial fault. It is a perversion of language itself. It does injustice to the social contract. No wonder that St. Augustine regarded lying as a grave sin, not merely because it corrupted the currency of speech, but because it placed itself in opposition to divine law. Robert Louis Wilkin summarizes the Augustinian view this way: "Mendacity prostitutes a precious gift of God—speech—the vehicle by which we are able to communicate with one another, to express our deepest thoughts and feelings, to enter into the mind of another person, to speak the truth to one another. Because God is truth and the source of truth, lying is a turning to self and away from

God, an offense against the Creator, speech driven by distorted desire." Though lying qualifies as one of the most serious of the perversions of language, there are a slew of lesser offenders, i.e., gossip, small talk, low slang and blasphemy. Of course, there are times in this cornucopia of usage when there are pleasant "poetic surprises," albeit just this side of slickness. The phonetically prone *Chicago Tribune* came up with this headline some years ago: STATE HIKES FRATE RATE. If we overlook the misspelling, we have a fine example of internal rhyme. Headline writers and PR types have been adopting poetic tropes for years to serve their purposes. We recall the slogan that helped to elect Dwight Eisenhower: I LIKE IKE. Likewise, automobile pitchmen have never had an aversion to alliteration, as in Lexus' "passionate pursuit of perfection."

In some journalism, a genuine poetic impulse manages to transcend what is habitually expected, as in this headline that announced the death of the Italian novelist, Alberto Moravia: *SENZA MORAVIA* (WITHOUT MORAVIA.). It may not have been journalistically correct, but it must have captured the pathos of that moment. Using the same headline technique after November 22, 1963 would undoubtedly have had a similar effect. Another classical example of a headline that was poetically inspired happened after Manolete, the greatest Spanish matador of the twentieth century, was fatally gored in the last *faena* of the last bullfight of the last tour of his life: *MATO MURIENDOSE, Y SE MURIO MATANDO* (HE KILLED DYING, AND HE DIED KILLING). Such unexpected poetry happens almost by accident, as if the ordinary diction of our lives finds itself unequal to the challenge. Slang has also been known to coin words or phrases that pinpoint their subjects more imaginatively than the proper nouns by which we know them: "sooner" instead of Oklahoman, "jock" instead of athlete, "roadside bomb" instead of improvised explosive device. As for blasphemy there is now no question that the usual four-letter words are overworked clichés. They seem almost childish when compared with this remarkable curse by Robert Desnos: "Cursed be the father of the bride of the blacksmith who forged the iron for the axe with which the oak was felled from which the bed was carved in which was conceived the great-grandfather of the man who was driving the carriage in which your mother met your father."

Because poetry is the language of felt thought and utterance ("a poet," said Ezra Pound, "is a man who, believing in silence, could not refrain from speaking"), of admissions and oaths as sacred as life itself, it is evident in an economy by its absence. As long as people are perceived in economic terms alone, poetry (and all the other arts, for that matter) will be regarded as ornamental or irrelevant and ultimately dispensable. However, if people are more than mere economic integers, then the disregard of poetry will be as fatal to their spiritual lives as the deprivation of oxygen would be to their physical lives. Why? Because poetry shows us who we are, what our surroundings means to us and what waits to be discovered beneath the apparent. In such ways poetry is our way of rendering justice to the world and our place in it. It is the language of the heart (by which we know ourselves and which, in Pascal's words, "has reasons that the reason does not know") and of the senses (through which we know the world).

To say that poetry is as essential to our spiritual lives as oxygen is to our physical lives is not a mere figure of speech. The fact is that human beings cannot deny their need to feel the full range of life's integral emotions any more than they can consider oxygen a mere option and not a necessity. People cannot live unfeelingly, however hard the stoic in them may try. Without meeting or even acknowledging their need for feeling, people are reduced to dullness, which is self-imposed solitary confinement. Such people become disassociated from the wellsprings of personal and social health. An economy, of course, is quite indifferent to that. It wants no more than a population composed of puritans of industry. The entire American capitalistic system is rooted in that. But the human spirit is not. It craves the solidarity of feeling. And feelings, as every human being must eventually admit, move inexorably toward expression. And who but poets—or any child or adult wen moved to say something in a poetic way —fulfill this need for themselves and for those who experience what they say fulfill this need in our society? It is one thing to say we create our lives by the decisions we make and that the outcomes are not known to us in advance. It is quite something else to say the same thing as Antonio Machado said it in two lines that are quoted throughout the Spanish-speaking world: *Caminante, no hay camino. Se hace camino al andar.* (Wayfarer, there is no road. You make the road as you go.)

True poems are momentary intensities, and they are invariably as brief as they are unforgettable. They startle us into the ongoing life of the present tense, and they keep us there are long as we are within their grip. Like the times of kisses and tears, they have no past or future tense. Like telegrams, they eschew the superfluous and treasure the vital. They emphasize the power of less, calling to mind the principle in physics that shows how reducing spatial volume increases the pressure in the reduced space. In poetic expression we strive for such succinctness. Gustave Flaubert expressed this beautifully when he claimed that "human speech is like a cracked kettle on which we tap crude rhythms for bears to dance to, while we long to make music that will melt the stars."

True poetic utterance is born of necessity coupled with reflection. It involves a stepping back and a perception of the passing moment as it is and not as it appears to be. In an economy where reality is often distorted to support an ulterior worldview or agenda, the goal is not to say what is true but what will breed compliance and keep the economy going. To serve such ends, language is often merchandised and cheapened, and what we are left with is a lie. Misused in this way, such corrupted language can lead and has led to everything from confusion to war, as our own recent history regrettably confirms. If poetry has no other claim to our attention, the fact that it has no truck with lies is sufficient justification for its value. And the men or women who are suddenly inspired to make such utterances need no further credential but the truth of what they are moved to express, as was the child before the unclothed emperor who simply said what was there—or, as it turned out, not there. "Wise words are rarer than emeralds," goes the ancient adage, "yet they come from the mouths of poor slave girls who turn the millstones." Such wise words have a necessary place in public life. They are visionary and sustain what is true amidst what passes. The poetic expressions of men and women who answer this call fulfill the mission that Nobel Laureate St. John Perse enjoined upon poets everywhere—to be "the guilty conscience of their time." In this way they can make us aware feelingly of what mattes and what does not. And in what Dylan Thomas called their "craft and art," they can confirm that truth will always outlive lies in the same way that love will always outlive death.

Most of the words we hear, speak or read every day create the language of flat prose. It passes as small talk, gossip or the daily collection of questions-and-responses that is called conversation. On television, radio and what's left of newsprint in competition with computer-driven prose the quality is pared down to language squeezed between sound bites or deadlines. In other areas where we should expect more, we invariably get less. Oratory, for example, or poetry? Only a minority avails itself of such. Some have said that the declining quality of our public discourse may be traceable to our weak reading habits. The late novelist Jerzy Kosinski discovered through research that the literate population (which is not synonymous with the total population) of the United States had not read a single book during the year previous. Of the remaining 50% approximately 35% had read only a single book. We are then left with 15% who read more than one book. And of these the number of those who read a book of poetry would be but a fraction of that.

In one of his many prophetic (in the real sense of "seeing the present") books the superb Uruguayan author Eduardo Galeano explained the roots of our dysfunctionalism in regard to what we say as follows: "From the moment we enter school or church, education chops us into pieces; it teaches us to divide soul from body and mind from heart. The fisherman of the Colombian coast must be learned doctors of ethics and morality. For they invented the word *sentipensante*, feeling/thinking, to define language that speaks the truth." The fishermen to whom he was referring told Galeano that the language of *sentipensante* was the only language worth hearing. Even in the most ordinary ways the need and preference for the language of *sentipensante* assert themselves. I was discussing with a young woman the absence of courses in handwriting or cursive in many curricula. A teacher herself, she nodded. I asked her what she thought of that. She shrugged indifferently. I then asked her, "Would you rather receive a love letter handwritten or emailed?" "Handwritten, of course," was her immediate answer. I then said, "But the email and the letter are both are saying the same thing." 'It's how it's said that matters," she answered and added, "the handwritten one would be more personal." Since then I have put the same question to a number of other women of varying ages, and not a single one voted for the email over the handwritten. I never mentioned to them the possibility that eliminating instruction in cursive from every curriculum would mean the end of their preferred love letters. There is even a physiological reason why handwritten letters or messages are by nature more personal than typewritten ones or push-button emails. A hand-held pen establishes a connection between the hand, heart and mind that mechanized alternatives cannot do. Perhaps it derives from the fact that letters of the alphabet are connected when written by hand while the same letters, when printed, are separated. In the order of oral expression, I have already noted the diminution of poetry and oratory as forces in our cultural and political lives.

Where the language of *sentipensante* should predominate we invariably hear only basic communication, if that. Even though the expression of precise feeling is far more diffi-cult than the expression of precise thought, those from whom such expression is expected often fail in their at-tempts or miss the point entirely. In addition, so much of contemporary American poetry is motivated not by what reveals our common humanity but by differences in gen-der, race, ethnicity, social status or age. The result is not literature but sociology. Also, many American poets, when reciting their poems in public, rarely recite from memory but read their poems as if they were recipes from a cook-book. Russian poets in the Yevtushenko tradition together with many similar poets from Europe and the Middle East do just the opposite so that what we witness are not po-etry readings but poetry hearings. From the 1960's to the present the language of *sentipensante* has been heard more in the voices of singers rather than poets or orators, not only in the United States but elsewhere in the world. Bob Dylan, Leonard Cohen, Joni Mitchell and Judy Collins have multiple admirers. Songs like "The Times They Are A'Changing," "Who Knows Where the Time Goes" and "Both Sides Now" have reached and moved millions. The Simon and Garfunkel soundtrack for *The Graduate* became a classic of its time and beyond. Many of the songs of Joan Baez in both English and Spanish are known to audiences from coast to coast. The public esteem that such singers earn reminds me historically of the French singer Edith Piaf and the esteem in which she was held by French audi-ences until she died. And the same can be said of the Greek singer Nana Mouskouri. She sings not only in Greek but in seven other languages, and her collective audience from her concerts and otherwise has been estimated to be the largest audience for a female singer in history. In Lebanon the fame of Julia Boutros has been compared to that of the legendary Egyptian singer Um Khaltum. When Um Khaltum died, it was said that more than four million came in tribute at her funeral in Cairo. Julia Boutros of Lebanon appears before thousands in outdoor concerts in Tyre and elsewhere, and the audiences can be seen standing and clapping and singing the songs along with her that she is singing to them. The music is felt, not simply heard. I do not mean to carry too far the observation that singers may be considered the poets of our time. I think Bob Dylan has written a number of good songs, but I do not think they are of Nobel Prize stature when compared with the poems of Nobel Awardees of the past, i.e. William Butler Yeats, Derek Walcott, Seamus Heaney, Wislawa Szymborska. The fact remains that Dylan wrote what people felt or wanted to feel. He and other singers filled the vacuum that many poets and orators could not fill. And that is where we find ourselves today.

Sturdily muscled and tattooed, he said his name was Tyler. He was one a crew who'd come to pave my neighbor's driveway. Having had my own driveway paved ten years before, I asked Tyler what the current price was. "I don't make the deals," Tyler responded, "I'm a labor person."

She was the organizer of the Moms (later joined by Disabled Veterans) who had come to support the protestors in Portland, Oregon. Having been teargassed the night before, she hesitated for a moment and then said, "My eyes burned, and I retched and vomited, and I couldn't control my body fluids."

Listening to news is often a waste of attention. Instead of simply being informed, we are confronted, assertion by assertion. The very character of news reporting in the spoken media is basically assertive. Inundated by assertions over the past four decades, we have ensconced a presidential actor, four not too dissimilar politicians and an affluent oaf. There's not an orator or stateman in the lot, and the ultimate recognition of our national decline over this period came at the conclusion of the Cohen public hearings when the chairman of the committee, Elijah Cummings, stated with undisguised passion, "We're better than this." The answer is unclear. Ideally, we are better. American sacrifice, generosity and valor have always come to the fore in times of crisis. Realistically, as the daily news abundantly asserts, we have much to correct in order to be better. A good starting point is education. In the words of Thomas Jefferson, John Dewey and numerous others, education is the bedrock of democracy since it makes possible an enlightened citizenry. Without education, democracy slides into decline. It is to forestall that decline that education becomes indispensable. The role of the teacher in this process is both obvious and pivotal. To witness teachers on strike, as is becoming more and more frequent, for better pay, benefits and working conditions is to identify administrative and public failure to anticipate and recognize these needs until they are brought to public attention. Teachers, on the whole, regard teaching not merely as a job but as calling—a vocation. Elementary and secondary school teachers, who teach five or more classes a day, realize that only a vocational dedication sustains them. Those who think otherwise should experience this regimen (plus time for daily preparation) for a single day to disabuse themselves of this illusion.

Consider the pivotal errors in American foreign policy that a self-educated person could inevitably identify as adventurism, first in Vietnam and later in Iraq. Both were presidentially initiated while Congress played "second fiddle," even though the Constitution stipulates that Congress alone can commit the country to war. The cultural history of Vietnam and Iraq was either little understood or ignored. The damage done to both is incalculable, and the deaths of the indigenous populations were numbered in the hundreds of thousands. Meanwhile our inclinations to invade or implant an American presence around the world has shown no signs of waning. We currently have 150,000 troops stationed in one hundred and seventy countries at a cost of twenty billon a year. Keeping troops in Afghanistan and Iraq alone costs approximately $472,000,000 a day. Citizens with a sense of history would not be wrong in asking if such implantations are in the best interest of the United States or if the soldiers stationed there understood the culture of the countries selected. In the case of Afghanistan and Iraq where deaths of Americans and indigenous inhabitants actually happened, a familiarity with history would have helped anyone understand why resistance to foreigners was predictable in both countries. It would also be logical for Americans to wonder if the consequences of a war identified by the instigator (George W. Bush) as the start of an endless war would have repercussions on American society itself.

Could recent American history have been different if political leadership had been influenced by more liberally educated officials and to what extent was liberal education found wanting or lacking in creating such leadership? Take my own University of Notre Dame as an example. In his memoir entitled *My Notre Dame*, Thomas Stritch, who was not only an alumnus but later a professor and chairman of Notre Dame's Department of Journalism, noted that more than 1,300 students out of a total population of 3,000 in the 1930's chose to major in the liberal arts. This is slightly less than 50%. Seventy-five to ninety years later the percentages changed markedly. In 2005 and 2006 the number of students majoring in four of the liberal arts (English, psychology, political science and history) was approximately 1,758 out of a student population of approximately 8,600. By 2021 the number of liberal arts majors was slightly more than 800 out of roughly the same total population number.

This is not completely surprising. There has been a general and regrettable decrease in the number of students majoring in the liberal arts nationally and even internationally. One of the reasons for this is the fallacious assumption that liberal arts majors are less immediately employable than those with a more "practical" major. A second and more pressing reason is that the costs of a higher education are so high now that students who are forced to borrow in order to meet such costs need to find work in a profession as soon as possible to repay their debts. This often inclines them to choose majors which they believe will assure them of employment as soon as possible after graduation. Majoring in history, philosophy or English is not high on their list.

There were also a variety of military considerations that did not allow collegians or collegians-to-be to make decisions about their majors. From 1950 on we have lived with one government after another that was inclined to initiate military interventions through presidential choice. The result of this was that American troops were a presence all over the world and that 85,000 service men and women lost their lives, and hundreds of thousands were wounded in more than seven chosen wars to date. The reaction against this began in the latter stages of the Vietnam War when soldiers on active duty along with thousands of college-age young men engaged in violent protests, culminating in the killing of protesting students at Kent State. Thinking that he could forestall further violent protests, Nixon ended the draft without discussing the pressing issues of war and peace that prompted the protests. But the disastrous wars went on regardless. Nixon and others seemed to believe that creating a private military would end further protests since protesting volunteers could simply be told, "As an enlistee you pledged to follow orders, so you're just doing what you enlisted to do when you confront civilian protestors to keep the peace."

The effect on students, the vast majority of whom were totally opposed to our actions in Vietnam and later invasions, was that many sought and received draft deferments because they were students. After the draft ended, some enlisted in the hope of benefiting from the G. I. Bill if they survived. Colleges and universities saw their enrollments remain the same in either case. The costs of a college education increased and increased until we reached a point where those who could afford to attend were either the children of the ultra-wealthy or the remaining vast majority who were faced with the inevitable burden of debt—some for the rest of their lives.

I leave further political, military and economic consequences of these matters to historians. My purpose in this essay is to consider their effect on higher education, particularly liberal education.

The root of the word "education" means "to lead out from." The student is one who is led out of or from himself by studying those subjects that interrupt his privacy and lead him to contemplate what is more than or other than himself. In practice this induces the student or the learner to discover what exceeds his own person. If continued, this leads to an endless search for the truth about the nature of man, which, finally, is the only way to fulfill the educational fundamental two-word command of Socrates —"Know thyself." This means more than knowing one's name, age and address. It means studying the nature of man as revealed in literature, history, political science and other fields where the truth is sought for its own sake. In the course of these studies the student is led to confront the *why* and not just the *how* of life. Such questions do not have categorical answers, and the very attempt to answer them can lead not only to self-knowledge but to the ways in which men have created societies and realized the need of law as an arbiter in community and world affairs.

Because the questions raised by the dispassionate pursuit of truth leads to discussion, learning in liberal arts classes transcends instruction. Inquiry and discussion are the norm, and inquiry and discussion between knowledgeable and honest students are the essence of education. Albert Jay Nock went as far as to say that only the "educable person" can pursue it. He believed that the resultant knowledge would emerge only in the "pursuit of truth." He dismissed other alternatives as training and added dismissively that "anybody can be trained."

Nock's views, though differing theologically, are in the direct tradition of those enunciated a century earlier by John Henry Cardinal Newman in *On the Scope and Nature of University Education*. Here, for example, is how Newman expressed the nature of a true education compared to its alternative: "You see then, gentlemen, here are two methods of education; the one aspires to be philosophical, the other to be mechanical; the one rises toward ideas, the other is exhausted upon what is particular and external. Let me not be thought to deny the necessity or to decry the benefit, of such attention to what is particular and practical, the useful and mechanical arts; life could not go on without them; we owe our daily welfare to them; their exercise is the duty of the many, and we owe to the many a debt of gratitude for fulfilling it. I only say that knowledge, in proportion as it tends more and more to be particular, ceases to be knowledge." Newman would probably identify such contemporary majors as Accounting, Finance and Applied and Computational Mathematics and Statistics as skills, not knowledge as he understands the term. Were he living at this moment he would undoubtedly say they have no place, despite their usefulness, in a college curriculum as he would define it.

Here is how Newman defines the basic challenges facing a student engaged in liberal education—an education whose goal is not train but to free the mind. "He (the student) profits from an intellectual tradition which is independent of particular teachers, which guides him in his choice of subjects, and duly interprets for him those which he chooses. He apprehends the great outlines of knowledge, the principles on which it rests, the scale of its parts, its lights and its shades, its great points and its little, as he otherwise cannot apprehend them. Hence it is that his education is called liberal. A habit of mind is formed which lasts through his life, of which the attributes are freedom, equitableness, calmness, moderation and wisdom; or what I have ventured to call a philosophical habit...This is the special fruit of the education furnished at a university."

Read any of the college catalogues of this and recent eras, and you will look long and hard to find echoes of Newman's vision. Instead, education is seen as preparation for professionalism of one kind or another without suggesting any larger purpose. It's small wonder that the late Dr. Robert Kibbee, once Chancellor of the City University of New York, said that college bulletins rank high in the romantic literature of our time. Currently, the purpose of four years of college is to meet a student's need to qualify for a job that society may need at that moment. The needs of society take priority over the creation of an independent habit of mind. In essence, society is seen as an economy, and students are regarded as the serviceable parts that exist to keep the economy running.

This is a disservice not only to the students but to the university and to society. Full participation of college graduates in a democratic society should be one of the major benefits of a college education, and liberally educated graduates with a philosophical habit of mind are the ideal participants. Challenges at the city, state, national and international level as well as ongoing personal concerns demand attention and the constant pursuit of truth. Escape into privacy is not an option but an escape. The root of the Greek word for "idiot" describes someone who turns his back on society and does not participate in public life.

The pursuit of truth has always been difficult, even in those circumstances where it is encouraged, as it is or should be on university and college campuses. But in our time, we live in a militarized nation in a militarized world. Resorting to resolving serious differences by force seems to be the preference of some who have the means to do so. This is suicidal. Intelligent men and women of peace must find ways to make intelligence prevail. The alternative could mean the end of humanity as we know it.

We have already had a preview of this challenge. The Cuban Missile Crisis was precipitated by Russia's installation of nuclear missile sites on the island of Cuba. While total militarists like General Curtis LeMay advocated bombing the sites to dust, President Kennedy opted for a blockade and diplomacy. Within thirteen days the crisis was resolved with Russia's removal of the missiles and their sites. Kennedy responded that the United States would not invade and that its own nuclear missile sites would be removed from Turkey in exchange, adding that any attack thereafter on any nation in the western hemisphere would be regarded as an attack on the United States. This exchange between Russia and the United States led to further discussions and eventually induced both nations to sign the Nuclear Test Ban Treaty. However unpopular Kennedy and his brother later became with many on the Joint Chiefs of Staff, the fact remains that diplomacy, patience and readiness eventually averted nuclear war.

If any future war would be waged by the most dominant powers, it is projected that on the first day of conflict, 34.1 million human beings would be killed and 57.1 million wounded. The United States and Russia, each having more than 3000 nuclear bombs apiece aimed at prime targets in each country, would be the chief destroyers. If war continued beyond the first day, it is estimated that more than 400 to 500 million would be killed and wounded. There would subsequently be 348 million casualties due to fallout or temperature change. In time there would also be some 772 million deaths or disabilities caused by poisonous soot in the atmosphere.

Faced with such an Apocalypse, one would think that any world leader would attempt to call mankind to reason. The only unforgettable speech on this subject was given by President John F. Kennedy in June of 1963 at the American University in Washington. It was an appeal for peace based on man's abhorrence of war, especially nuclear war. After Barack Obama's installation in the presidency in 1980, when he had already been awarded the Nobel Peace Prize, he could have made a similar speech to emphasize the gravity of the moment. Instead, he ordered 30,000 more troops into Afghanistan to continue the universally opposed war initiated by Bush *fils*. He emphasized force, not reason, and the results continue to be ruinous. Perhaps that is why that war that began with the invasion of Iraq in 2003 was protested nationally and internationally by more people than ever in the total history of war resistance.

I mention these historical moments not for political reasons but only to heighten the relevance of the philosophical mind to all aspects of our lives on this planet. The relevance of this to our lives in times of peace needs no further elaboration. A philosophical mind in pursuit of truth makes all other considerations secondary—not ignorable but secondary. Conflicts rooted on race, status or gender, for example, are secondary to what is of common concern to all of us as human beings. Nuclear war is the common enemy of all. Opposed to that are the liberal arts, which stand for what is primary—the pursuit of truth and intellectual freedom. The continued existence of universities as universities in this dangerous world depends upon that.

The continued existence of the human race depends upon that.

Is there a connection between the violence in American cities like Chicago and Baltimore and the fact that our country has been involved in war for two decades, that we have become inured to death counts, that the popular arts like motion pictures and television, often re-create this violence replete with special effects? More importantly has the very possibility of peace, cooperation and leisure been so reduced in importance that we no longer regard them as ideals. If this is true, then the political and cultural dimension of our lives is reduced to permanent competition. At some levels this has lethal consequences. Consider the number of homicides and suicides that occur annually in our country compared with other countries. In 2018 there were more than 20,000 homicides, mostly by gun, in the United States. During the same period there were 22 homicides in Japan. Owning a gun or a sword is illegal in Japan. All the current debate about Second Amendment rights seems irrelevant in light of the numerous murders that would not have happened here if guns were not available. The same could be said of suicides by gunshot, which numbered some twenty per day in 2018. Most of these were the suicides of veterans, and it is not presumptuous to assume that their physical or psychological wounds from their involvement in war might have had something to do with that. Turning to matters domestic, are our social and cultural lives better than they were in the 1950's, 1960's or 1970's? Cell phones now can interrupt the most intimate or crucial conversations at will. Formal etiquette, manners and basic courtesy—especially to women—is regarded as superfluous. Equality of opportunity now extends even to the infantry. In this and similar areas one is inclined to agree with Nobel Awardee Marguerite Yourcenar's rather obvious reservation, "Equality is not identity." And, finally there is the priority given to hand-held computers or other devices during person-to-person encounters so that actual conversation, which, like sleep, can only be beneficial when it is uninterrupted, never really happens. I leave aside for the moment the preponderance of tattoos as a sign of...of what? Exhibitionism, body art, freedom, conformity, rebellion? Who knows? And there is a kind of deliberate casualness in dress. I remember having dinner in a good but not consciously upperclass restaurant where one man in a T-shirt was dining with his rather well-dressed wife.

Consider for a moment the slavishness of fashion. Sometimes it is merely a variation from the ordinary, i.e., the habit of men sporting stubble whiskers or beards in lieu of being shaven. If someone says that the beard actually conceals the face, the remark can be seen as regressive or an affront to personal preference. If a beard, incipient or full, is taken as a sign of excessive virility, that's really giving hair a lot more power than it deserves, Samson notwithstanding. Regardless, what suddenly becomes fashionable or simply a matter of preference can be seized upon by those obsessed with group behavior to create larger numbers of national or international followers with consequences that have unforeseeable social and economic dimensions. Take the current fad among adolescents of both sexes to wear denim trousers or jeans that are slit one or more times at the knees. For some reason the "slit jean" has become an essential part of a teenager's wardrobe. Seizing on this, some clothing manufacturers began pro-

ducing jeans that were sold "pre-slit." I have not re-
searched this, but it is my understanding that these pre-
slit jeans are priced higher than those that are not. What
else but an exploitation of quirky adolescent taste can explain this. The same kind of contagious imitation may be
behind the inclination of many to sport tattoos. Of course,
it is any person's right to tattoo his or her body. But in
essence such widespread tattooing is nothing but a form
of exhibitionism. It comes down to inking the skin in various patterns or shapes so that they can be seen. I can
think of no more determined and ongoing attempt to
bring people under its sway than the efforts of the National Rifle Association vis-à-vis "gun rights." For the moment let's put aside the pro and con allusions to the Second Amendment. The Amendment had its strongest influence when controlled "militias" were the order of the day,
but it has since been invoked to justify "pistol packing" in
plain sight, which has brought us back to images of Dodge
City and "Guns Along the Pecos." But tabling discussion of
the Amendment for the moment, it is revealing to compare gun-deaths in the United States (homicides plus suicides per year) with those of other countries, particularly
with Japan, where owning a gun or a sword is illegal and
where permission to own a weapon (but never a hand-
gun) is accompanied with compulsory class attendance.
Japan has a population of approximately 127,000,000.
Gun deaths in Japan in 2017, exclusive of suicides, came to
22. The number of deaths by gun in the United States in
2017 was slightly below 40,000. Numbers were similar on
2018. The obvious but ignored conclusion that can be
drawn from this is that gun deaths in both countries were
directly proportionate to the availability of firearms. This
is not speculation but directly supported by the facts. All

pro and con arguments related to the Second Amendment
pale in importance in relation to that.

Consider Ralph Nader's forthright challenge of the automobile industry vis-à-vis seat belts. We have long since accepted the truth that seat belts save lives. For years they
have been installed in all cars nationally (and internationally), and drivers can be cited if they are spotted with seat
belts unfastened. Corporate resistance to seat belts was
unrelenting from the first time Nader publicly spoke
about their necessity. He was ridiculed, disparaged and
slandered. There were even insinuations about his private
life as the manufacturers realized that his arguments were
beginning to sway the public. Eventually the truth pre-
vailed. In retrospect how many lives were lost before seat
belts were made mandatory? How many lives have been
saved since then? And, above all, how much is owed to
Ralph Nader who persisted in his "disobedience" until the
truth was impossible to ignore or deny.

In his last book, *Dear Zealots*, the late Israeli novelist and
essayist Amos Oz explored the political consequences of
mindless following in merciless detail: "The urge to follow
the crowd and the passion to belong to the majority are
fertile ground for fanatics, as are the various cults of personality, idolization of religious and political leaders, and
the adulation of entertainment and sports celebrities. Of
course, there is a great distance between blindly worship-
ing bloodthirsty tyrants, being swept up in murderous
ideological or aggressive, hateful chauvinism, and the
inane adoration of celebrities. Still, there is perhaps a
common thread: the worshiper yields his own selfhood.
He longs to merge—to the point of self-deprecation—with

the throng of other admirers and unite with the experiences and accomplishments of the object of worship. In both cases, the elated admirer is subjugated by a sophisticated system of propaganda and brainwashing, a system that intentionally addresses the childish elements in people's souls, the element that so longs to merge, to crawl back into the warm womb, to once again be a tiny cell inside a huge body, a strong and protective body—the nation, the church, the movement, the party, the team fans, the groupies—to belong, to squeeze in with a crowd under the broad wings of a great father, an admired hero, a dreamy beauty, a sparkling celebrity, in whose hands the worshipers deposit their hopes and dreams, and even their right to think and judge and take positions."

The late Tony Judt stated in his last book *Ill Fares the Land*, "Much of what appears 'natural' today dates from the 1980's: obsession with wealth, the cult of privatization and the private sector, the growing disparities of rich and poor, and, above all, the rhetoric that accompanies the uncritical admiration for unfettered markets...and the delusion of endless growth." For Tony Judt as well as for Robert Reich, the root of the problem is spiritual. As a people and as a government, we are now less altruistic, more self-concerned, more acquisitive and less generous. In the sixties, building on the New Deal's creation of Social Security and the GI Bill of Rights, there was, as already noted, the Kennedy-initiated and the Johnson-shepherded agenda of Medicare, Medicaid, the Civil Rights Act, food stamps, Headstart, the National Endowment for the Arts, the National Endowment for the Humanities, the Peace Corps, student loans and the Corporation for Public Broadcasting. All of these could truthfully be described as being for the public good and in the public interest. There has been no comparable legislation since then. The epigraph from the poetry of Alexander Pope that Judt chose for his last book says more about us now than most would like to admit: "Ill fares the land, to hastening ills a prey,/ Where wealth accumulates, and men decay."

In July of 2006 there had been an incursion at the border of Lebanon and Israel in which some Israeli soldiers had been captured. Such incidents were not uncommon and were often resolved by negotiations or swaps. This time the Israeli government of Prime Minister Ehud Olmert opted for war against the entirety of Lebanon. In 2006 the Israelis attacked the country's airport, the national infrastructure (bridges, roads etc.), power stations, the towns and villages of southern Lebanon, a coastal oil refinery whose oil spill fouled the coasts and beaches of Lebanon, Syria and Turkey for years and culminated finally in the dropping of thousands of cluster bombs that would claim and indeed have already claimed the lives of numerous children from 2006 to the present. Numerically the cost in human lives in Lebanon was over 1000. The number of wounded was incalculable, and over 150,000 inhabitants were displaced. Every member of the United Nations, with the exception of the United States, Israel and Great Britain, was on record on the third day of the war that it should be stopped. The Israeli government claimed that it was responding to terror. By punishing the country and population as a whole, it hoped to turn the people against their government. This is a rationale it has used for decades. The most recent example was the country-wide assault on Gaza by land, sea and air in 2014, resulting in the deaths of 2015 Gazans, including 495 children and 253 women.

At that time, Likud spokesman Eli Hazan said of the Gazans near the border, "All 30,000 are legitimate targets."

For years I had been an admirer of John Ciardi—as a poet, an essayist in *The Saturday Review*, a television commentator and a public intellectual. Over the years he had even accepted a poem or two of mine for the review. What was and still is a mystery to me is why Ciardi is not included in anthologies of contemporary American poets. I don't know if it's an ethnic bias or not, but this omission demands correction. His love poems are exceptional as are his poems on what can be called "the American scene" in the poem that begins "In the next election, if I am elected..." In any event, he accepted the invitation to appear at the Forum. He drew a capacity audience and semi-read-and-recited his poems in the same concentrated tone that characterized his talks with me—no posturing, no fluff, no theatrics. At one point he recalled an incident in his boyhood when he was reprimanded and sent home from school. (It was his preface to the reciting of a poem whose title I've forgotten.). Later on the same day a priest came to his home to follow up on the reprimand. Ciardi's mother answered the door, confronted the priest before he could say a word and said, "You leave my Johnny alone, you Irish you." After the reading, he told me over coffee that his forbears came to the United States from central Italy, near Naples. Ethnically he added that north of Rome historically the population's roots were Germanic while south of Rome the origins were Greek. He said that etymology of Ciardi was Gerhardt, which evolved into Gerardi and eventually into Ciardi.

In the late nineteen sixties I was invited by the State Department to present a series of poetry programs in Lebanon, Jordan, Egypt and Greece. Greece would be the final stop on the tour with lectures in Athens and Thessaloniki. As soon as my wife and I arrived in Athens, we were told that George Seferis (Seferiadis), the Nobel Laureate for literature, would be presenting his poems in the American Hellenic Union on the night before my scheduled appearance there. Seferis's program would be the first time his countrymen would have an opportunity to hear him since the award was announced. By that time Seferis was known throughout the world. Having Seferis recite his poems in Greece before his fellow Greeks was an event whose significance could not be minimized. I asked our host if it would be possible for us to see and meet him, and he said he would work for that to happen on the following day. By the time the evening of the following day was upon us, Athens was in a state of celebration. Every seat in the auditorium of the American Hellenic Union was occupied. Loudspeakers had been mounted outside the building so that the overflow crowd could *their* poet. Our host told us that it would be wiser to meet Seferis before he made his remarks because those who would come backstage afterward would make even a short conversation with Seferis impossible. And so, we followed him to the auditorium where Seferis and his wife were waiting for us in as guest room backstage. Seferis was of moderate height, and the serious cast of his features gave me the immediate impression that he was a man given to pondering. And like a man given to formality (he had been Greece's ambassador to various countries, including Lebanon which we had only just visited) he was wearing a vest. Someone had prepared him for the meeting by telling him that I was a writer visiting Greece under the auspices of the Department of State.

"Where did you speak before coming to Greece?" Seferis asked.

"Beirut, Amman, Jerusalem and Cairo."

"Ah, Beirut," he said with half a smile, "I was posted there for several years."

"I read your *Levant Journal*. You describe your time in the country in detail there."

Seferis nodded and then asked, "Did you recite your poems in the countries you visited?"

I said that I did.

"In English?"

"Yes."

"Ah, you Americans," Seferis said and sighed. "You can go anywhere in the world and recite your poems in your own language and be understood." He paused. "I can only do that in my own country."

I had long been an admirer of the Greek actress Irene Papas. Her performance in *Zorba the Greek* was particularly memorable. At some point I began wondering if she would consider an invitation to appear at the Forum in a one-woman show built around the monologues of classical Greek heroines like Medea. Somehow I found a way to contact her and learned from her that she would be in New York and that we could meet at that time and discuss it further. After she gave me the date as well as the address, I flew to New York with my wife and five-year-old son, and all three of us proceeded to the address that she had given to me on the phone. She was waiting for us at the door of the apartment. She had the same taciturn beauty in person that she had on screen. She greeted us,

then turned her total attention to our son, who was holding my hand. "Come to me, baby," she said and opened her
arms to him, but he shied away while still holding my
hand. She continued to smile, came closer to him and ca-
ressed him briefly but tenderly. Then she led us into her
apartment and made us comfortable. With her attention
still on our son, she asked me to explain what I had in
mind for a program. I answered that I hoped she would
come and give a one-woman performance of monologues
that I would script from an assortment of classical Greek
dramas. She listened and then slowly but definitely shook
her head no.

"You want me to be all those crazy ladies?" she asked.

"Yes," I answered. "I can think of no other actress who
could do it."

"I cannot," she said finally. I thought my best response
was to say nothing.

She waited a moment and then said to me in the voice
of an actress, "When Mr. Cacoyannis is directing me, and
the audience is *they*, then I can perform. I am then in a
role, in character. But when I face the audience, and the
audience becomes *you*, I cannot. I hope you understand."

We stayed a bit longer, and she continued to try to get
our son's attention.

"Do you have children, Ms. Papas?" I asked.

"No," she answered. "No children. I am married one
time and a half."

I thought it wise not to pursue that.

Archibald MacLeish was an unignorable presence in the
literary world of the twentieth century as a poet, drama-
tist, attorney, man of state, essayist, public intellectual and
speaker. Perhaps it was these roles that created in him a

stature that was unique., Vanity had nothing to do with it. In his public appearances he always revealed a sense of the man he was without embellishment or hauteur. And unlike the public behavior of many literary figures, he always had a sense of occasion. Although I had never met him, I felt that Archibald MacLeish would be the ideal poet to launch the International Poetry Forum. I wrote him at his home in Conway, Massachusetts, and he answered that he would be honored to do so, and he did in the Fall of 1966. The Carnegie Lecture Hall was filled to capacity, and a hundred or so had to be turned away in the rain. Before reciting a selection of his poems, MacLeish stated that the Forum could not help but be of benefit to the city as well as to poetry itself simply by letting poetry speak for itself and become an accepted and expected part of public speech.

MacLeish returned on two subsequent occasions to the Forum. In 1978 the Forum presented a play that I personally commissioned. MacLeish had told me that had been spending a great deal of time reading the archived papers of John Adams and Thomas Jefferson and was envisioning some way of using them as the core of a dramatic dialogue between them. Eventually this evolved into MacLeish's last play, *The Great American Fourth of July Parade*, which we presented in the Carnegie Music Hall under the direction of John Housman with Melvyn Douglas and George Grizzard. It was later published by the University of Pittsburgh Press.

One casual incident stays with me from that experience. During one of the rehearsals, John Housman, who directed the production in a manner reminiscent of his direction of MacLeish's first radio play, *The Fall of the City*, asked Douglas if he would move his stage position a bit more to

Housman's left. Douglas smiled semi-politically and said, "Exactly where I have always stood, John, as long as we've known one another."

Years later during a visit to Conway where MacLeish and I were recording a conversation that would later be distributed on National Public Radio. I discussed with him his friendship with Ernest Hemingway. He began by showing me a copy for *A Farewell To Arms* inscribed by Hemingway to him. This led to a discussion of Paris and how the city became the residence for choice of many Americans as well as other Europeans in the years following World War I. MacLeish himself had given up a lucrative future as a partner in a Boston law firm to move to Paris with his wife, who was an accomplished singer and became a student of the legendary Nadia Boulanger while there. I asked him what attraction did Paris hold for so many talented people at that time. He said that the intellectual and cultural climate was a once-in-a-lifetime happening and that the cost of living was not only affordable but cheap. When MacLeish returned to the United States, he heard that Hemingway had been injured in a hunting accident in Montana. Because they had become close friends by then, MacLeish travelled by train from New York to Montana. In those days such a trip took days. When MacLeish arrived in Montana and went to the hospital, Hemingway asked him curtly, "Did you come to see me die?"

Among MacLeish's closest friends in New England was the legendary teacher (at Columbia), essayist and poet Mark Van Doren. Van Doren and MacLeish met frequently just to converse. At one point a trade publisher recorded their conversations and published them in a book called *The Dialogues of Archibald Macleish and Mark Van Doren*. The give and take in the dialogues revealed not only their agreements and occasional differences but validated a principle that Van Doren affirmed in his autobiography: "Friends do not have to agree on everything, but they have to have the same heroes and think the same men fools."

Bingo O'Malley was a versatile actor in Pittsburgh and elsewhere for many years, and his death was a loss for all of us who knew and admired and loved him. He opened several Forum programs as a reciter, and he also had the lead role in a play of mine called *Until I'm Not Here Anymore*. People often asked him if his real name was Bingo, and he answered that it truly was because his father was an admirer of Bing Crosby. On one occasion his name created an unexpected response. Bingo had taken his dog to a vet for a minor problem and left him there. Hours later he received a phone call, "Mr. O'Malley, your dog Bingo is ready."

W. D. Snodgrass's first book, *Heart's Needle*, was awarded the Pulitzer Prize. The book revealed a writer more assertive than suggestive but with a definite maturity. Included in this book was a poem entitled "April Inventory." There was a line in the poem that solidified his popularity—"...have eased a woman so she came." I remember his reading at the Forum as competent and thankfully audible, but what stays with me was his comment after our dinner together prior to the reading that he needed a little time before the reading to "tune his lute." I have no idea now what that meant.

I knew that Peter Ustinov was an accomplished actor. I knew also that he was intelligent and a man of independent thought. I don't recall how I made contact with him in order to extend my invitation. He was acting in a play in Toronto at the time. As part of the invitation, I explained that I could have him flown to Pittsburgh in a private plane. I added that he could write his own script and that it should include poems of his choice. It turned out to be the most original and outstanding performance I ever witnessed. Ustinov went from anecdote to anecdote in a variety of accents, occasionally quoting relevant poems. The only flaw in the performance was his inclusion of the poems of John Donne. He recited the poems flawlessly. It was evident that Ustinov had a genuine love of Donne's work. The problem was that he overestimated his audience. People listened closely out of respect for Donne himself and also for Ustinov, but they never seemed to be involved in the life of the poems they were hearing. Regardless, they applauded.

A man and woman who love one another by choice do so out of need. Each of them realizes that they are incomplete without each other though they cannot explain why. This does not weaken or nullify the desire they feel for each other but intensifies it. This is the essence of conjugal love..

If desire alone is the bond between a man and a woman, that means that it will be finite. The common adjectives applied to such relationships are usually associated with heat or fire. Marguerite Yourcenar in her short novel *Coup de Grace* portrays a couple so smitten by using images of fire to describe their feelings for one another. She then adds presciently that fire has only two destinies—to burn and to burn out.

"He always insisted that poetry should be read with the ear."

La Rochefoucauld: "Our real worth earns the respect of knowledgeable people, luck that of the crowd."

Sebastian Maniscalco, speaking of tattoos on the human body: "You don't put bumper stickers on a Ferrari."

Poetry has no past tense. Nor does music. Nor does God.

SAMUEL HAZO

The author of books of poetry, fiction, essays and plays, Samuel Hazo is the founder and director of the International Poetry Forum in Pittsburgh, Pennsylvania. He is also McAnulty Distinguished Professor of English Emeritus at Duquesne University, where he taught for forty-three years. From 1950 until 1957 he served in the United States Marine Corps, (Regular and Reserve), completing his tour as a captain. He earned his Bachelor of Arts degree magna cum laude from the University of Notre Dame, a Master of Arts degree from Duquesne University and his doctorate from the University of Pittsburgh. Some of his previous works are The Less Said, the Truer, The Next Time We Saw Paris, And the Time Is, Like a Man Gone Mad and Sexes: The Marriage Dialogues (Poetry), I Want It to Happen, The Time Remaining and If Nobody Calls, I'm Not Home (Fiction), Tell It to the Marines (Drama), The Stroke Of A Pen and Outspokenly Yours (Essays), Smithereened Apart (Critique of the poetry of Hart Crane), The Pittsburgh That Stays Within You (Memoir awarded the 2018 IPPY national bronze citation for creative non-fiction) and The World Within the Word: Maritain and the Poet (Critique). His translations include Denis de Rougemont's The Growl of Deeper Waters, Nadia Tueni's Lebanon: Twenty Poems for One Love and Adonis' The Pages Of Day And Night. In 2003 a selective collection of his poems, Just Once, received the Maurice English Poetry Award. He has been awarded twelve honorary doctorates. He was honored with the Griffin Award for Creative Writing from the University of Notre Dame, his alma mater, and was chosen to receive his tenth honorary doctorate from the university in 2008. A National Book Award finalist, he was named Pennsylvania's first State Poet by Governor Robert Casey in 1993, and he served until 2003.